SRA
Reading
Mastery
Signature Edition

Literature Guide
Grade 3

Siegfried Engelmann
Susan Hanner

SRA

Columbus, OH

Contents

SRAonline.com

Copyright © 2008 by SRA/McGraw-Hill.

Printed in the United States of America.

Send all inquiries to this address:
SRA/McGraw-Hill
4400 Easton Commons
Columbus, OH 43219

ISBN: 978-0-07-612588-3
MHID: 0-07-612588-2

3 4 5 6 7 8 9 10 MAZ 13 12 11 10 09 08

Introduction

The Literature Guide consists of 15 literature lessons, blackline masters that are to be reproduced as student material, and directions for the lessons. Literature activities are scheduled as part of every tenth lesson, starting with Lesson 10. In addition, there are two supplementary novels with questions and blackline masters. These two books may be presented after students have completed lesson 140 in *Reading Mastery Signature Edition*, Grade 3.

The following is a list of the selections and the lessons in which they are to be presented.

Literature Selections

Presented with Lesson	Title	Author
10	*The Velveteen Rabbit*	Harriet Winfield
20	*Dreams*	Langston Hughes
	The Runner	Faustin Charles
30	*The Emperor's New Clothes*	Harvey Cleaver
40	*Why Leopard Has Black Spots*	Told by Won-Ldy Paye
50	*Boar Out There*	Cynthia Rylant
	Crossing the Creek	Laura Ingalls Wilder
60	*Camp on the High Prairie*	Laura Ingalls Wilder
	Spaghetti	Cynthia Rylant
70	*Charlie Best*	Ruth Corrin
80	*The Pancake Collector*	Jack Prelutsky
90	*Not Just Any Ring*	Danita Ross Haller
100	*A Lucky Thing*	Alice Schertle
	The New Kid	Mike Makley
110	*Steps*	Deborah M. Newton Chocolate
120	*The Soup Stone*	Retold by Maria Leach
	Julie Rescues Big Mack	Roger Hall
130	*Amelia Bedelia*	Peggy Parish
135	*My (Wow!) Summer Vacation*	Susan Cornell Poskanzer
140	*The Story of Daedalus and Icarus*	Fran Lehr
Supplementary Novels	*The Chalk Box Kid* *Pirate Island Adventure*	Clyde Robert Bulla Peggy Parish

The Velveteen Rabbit tells how a young boy's love for his stuffed toy rabbit transforms the rabbit.

Dreams is a poem that tells why a person should hold on to dreams.

The Runner is a poem that compares the speed of a running man to the speed of other things.

The Emperor's New Clothes is the tale of a vain king who is tricked into wearing clothes that don't exist.

Why Leopard Has Black Spots is an African fable that teaches that a liar usually gets caught and pays a penalty.

Boar Out There tells how a young girl is afraid of and yet fascinated by a wild boar that lives in the woods near her home.

"Crossing the Creek" and *"Camp on the High Prairie"* are chapters from *Little House on the Prairie* that tell about a pioneer family's trip across the prairie.

Spaghetti explains that everyone needs something special to love to make life worthwhile.

Charlie Best is about the importance of backing a story with evidence when nobody believes you're telling the truth.

The Pancake Collector is a poem about an unusual collection.

Not Just Any Ring tells of a girl's lesson in wishing for "good days."

A Lucky Thing is a poem about some chickens and a robin that see each other's place in the world as a lucky thing.

The New Kid is a poem about a terrific new player on a kids' baseball team.

Steps is a story about two stepbrothers who end up being friends after having to deal with a mutual problem.

The Soup Stone demonstrates that with a little help from everyone, great things can be accomplished.

Julie Rescues Big Mack is a story about a young girl who saves the life of a friend's kidnapped dog.

Amelia Bedelia is a funny story about how directions can be misinterpreted.

My (Wow!) Summer Vacation shows how the things you think you won't like can actually end up being the most fun.

The Story of Daedalus and Icarus is a play based on a Greek myth that demonstrates consequences of disobedience.

Presenting the Lessons

Each literature lesson is based on a theme from the selection. The following chart lists the lesson themes and gives a brief summary of the primary expansion activities for each lesson.

Themes and Activities

Literature Lesson	Presented with Lesson	Theme	Primary Expansion Activities
1. *The Velveteen Rabbit*	10	Love	Students write about their favorite "soft and cuddly."
2-1. *Dreams*	20	Dream metaphors	Students make up additional parts of the poem; students draw pictures of dreams.
2-2. *The Runner*	20	Fantastic ability	Students draw a picture about running fast.
3. *The Emperor's New Clothes*	30	Admitting the truth	Students write a sequel to the story.
4. *Why Leopard Has Black Spots*	40	Deceit	Students write and illustrate a story about how another animal got its stripes; students create pictures that demonstrate animal camouflage.
5-1. *Boar Out There*	50	Fear	Students produce a map of the story; students discuss the story characters' fears; students write about their own fear.
5-2. (Read to) *Crossing the Creek**	50*	Fear	None
6-1. (Read to) *Camp on the High Prairie**	60*	Being safe	None
6-2. *Spaghetti*	60	What makes life worthwhile	Students discuss the changes in how the main character feels through the story; students write about the kind of place they'd like to live in.
7. *Charlie Best*	70	What's the evidence?	Students write a new "chapter" for the story, following established patterns of the story characters.
8. *The Pancake Collector*	80	Collections	Students write about a collection they would like to have.
9. *Not Just Any Ring*	90	Courage	Students research Native Americans of the southwest; students make clay models of different story locations.

10-1. *A Lucky Thing*	100	Perspective	Students write about things that might make somebody look lucky to somebody else.
10-2. *The New Kid*	100	Gender equality	None
11. *Steps*	110	Overcoming differences	Students write a play about characters who disagree about something; students discuss the relative importance of little problems when a big problem occurs.
12-1. *The Soup Stone*	120	Combined efforts; big changes can happen in small steps.	Students develop a recipe that involves an ingredient that doesn't change what the recipe produces; students discuss the group effort demonstrated in the story; students write an ending to a story that involves a group effort.
12-2. (Read to) *Julie Rescues Big Mack**	120*	Clues; mistreating animals	Students discuss potential behavior outcomes for the animal character and how the human characters can help the animal; students discuss story clues.
13. *Amelia Bedelia*	130	Unclear instructions	Students draw pictures for different interpretations of a set of unclear instructions.
14. *My (Wow!) Summer Vacation*	135	Achieving personal goals	Students write about their favorite vacation; students produce a map for the story.
15. *The Story of Daedalus and Icarus*	140	Disobedience	Students make or gather props, stage settings and costumes, and then put on a reading version of the play.

* Note that selections 5-2, 6-1, and 12-2 are "Read to" selections that do not appear in the student literature anthology but are in the back of this guide. They may be presented at a later time.

Time Requirements

Literature lessons are scheduled every ten lessons, starting with Lesson 10. The literature lesson is scheduled to follow each tenth lesson test. The literature lesson does not have to be scheduled on the same day as the test, and it should not be scheduled as part of the regular reading lesson. The literature lessons are a treat. Schedule each activity for 40-80 minutes.

Materials

In addition to the anthologies and the blackline masters, students need specific materials for the scheduled activities. The teacher material consists of this teacher presentation book which specifies for each lesson what materials are needed. (The major supplies that you'll need for these lessons are lined paper, crayons, scissors, tape, and paste.)

Preparation

Before presenting each literature lesson, read the scheduled activity, secure the materials, and run off the blackline masters.

Bibliography of Correlated Trade Literature

At the back of this guide, you will find a bibliography of correlated trade literature that

- lists every *Reading Mastery Signature Edition* grade 3 story selection.
- notes the lessons in which the story is presented.
- identifies a theme suggested by the story.
- recommends trade books that relate to the suggested theme.
- denotes the genre of each trade book.

The Velveteen Rabbit

Written by Harriet Winfield

Illustrated by José Miralles

Theme: Love

The Velveteen Rabbit tells how a young boy's love for his stuffed toy rabbit transforms the rabbit.

Materials Needed for Lesson

1 copy of the literature anthology for each student
1 copy of blackline masters 1A and 1B for each student
Lined paper

Presenting the Lesson

1. (Make copies of blackline masters 1A and 1B.)
2. (Distribute copies of blackline masters to students. Direct students to read orally the words in columns 1 and 2 of part A. Explain what the words mean.)

- (Teacher reference:)

1	2
1. cuddly	1. search
2. receive	2. snuggle
3. shabby	3. tattered
4. princess	4. velveteen

- Things that are **cuddly** make you feel good when you hold them. Stuffed animals are soft and cuddly.
- When you **get** something from somebody, you **receive** it. Here's another way of saying **He got a phone call from somebody: He received a phone call.** Here's another way of saying **He got a letter: He received a letter.**
- Something that is **shabby** is not neat and clean. An old run-down house is shabby.
- A **princess** is the daughter of a king and queen.
- When you **search** for something, you look carefully for it. Here's another way of saying **She looked carefully for her lost dog: She searched for her lost dog.**
- When you **snuggle** up to someone, you get as close as you can to the person.

- Clothing that is **tattered** is in bad shape and is falling apart. A coat that is in really bad shape is a tattered coat.
- **Velveteen** is a soft, shiny material that is like fur. It feels nice to pet something made of velveteen.

3. (Direct students to read orally the words in columns 3 and 4.)
- (Teacher reference:)

3
1. searched
2. received
3. snuggled
4. remembered
5. stuffing

4
1. shabbier
2. birthday
3. Timmy
4. bunny
5. bunnies
6. months

4. (Direct students to read the story aloud, calling on individual students to read two or three sentences at a time. Tell students to raise their hand and ask a question about anything in the story that they don't understand.)

5. (After students have completed the story, direct them to write answers to the questions in part B of blackline master 1A.)

(Answer Key:)
1. How old was Timmy when he got the velveteen rabbit? *4*
2. What color was the rabbit? *Pink.*
3. What did the rabbit look like after Timmy had it a few years?
   Ideas: *Gray, tattered, shabby.*
4. Who thought that Timmy should get rid of the velveteen rabbit?
   Idea: *His mother.*
5. In Timmy's dream, who told him something about his rabbit? *A princess.*
6. What did that person say would happen to the rabbit?
   Idea: *It would become a real rabbit.*
7. Where did his mother tell him to take the tattered rabbit?
   Idea: *Into the woods.*
8. When Timmy looked back at the rabbit, how had it changed?
   Idea: *It was a real rabbit.*

Retelling the Story

1. I'm going to call on individual students to retell different parts of this story. Who wants to start with the title and tell the first part of the story? (Call on a student. After the student has told the first part of the story, call on another student to start there and tell more of the story. Continue until the story has been retold. Praise accounts that present the important details of the story.)
2. (Repeat the procedure, calling on individual students.)

Optional—New Ending

- Raise your hand if you can tell the story with a different ending. (Call on a student.) Start where Timmy has a dream and tell the new ending.

Optional—Dramatization

- What part of the story do you like the best? (Call on individual students.)
- (Select one of the scenes.) Let's act out that part. (Assign students to play the roles of the characters and act out the selected scene.)

Literary Elements

1. Find part C on your worksheet. ✔
- I'll read what it says in the box. Follow along.
  All stories have three main elements. They are the **setting,** the **characters,** and the **plot.** Listen again: the three main elements are the setting, the characters, and the plot. Everybody, what are the three main elements? (Signal.) *The setting, the characters, and the plot.*

2. The **setting** is where and when the story takes place. Maybe the setting is in the city; maybe it's in a shack on a mountain. The setting may be some time in the future, or a hundred years ago.
- You read the story of the velveteen rabbit. Where does the first part of that story take place? (Call on a student. Idea: *Timmy's house.*)
- That's the setting. If the story took place at one time, that time would be part of the setting. Remember, the setting is where and when the story takes place. Everybody, say that rule about the setting. Get ready. (Signal.) *The setting is where and when the story takes place.*

3. The **characters** are the important people, animals, or objects that do things in the story. The main character is the main person or animal in the story. In the story about the velveteen rabbit, one of the main characters is not a person. What is it? (Call on a student. Idea: *A toy rabbit.*)
- Everybody, what's the name of the other main character? (Signal.) *Timmy.*
- Who are some of the other characters in the story? (Call on a student. Idea: *Timmy's mother, the princess.*)
- Those characters are not **main** characters.
- Everybody, is Santa Claus a character in the story about the velveteen rabbit? (Signal.) *No.*
- Remember, the characters are the persons, animals, or objects that do things in the story.

4. The **plot** is what happens to the characters in the story. What is the plot? (Signal.) *What happens to the characters in the story.*
- When you tell the plot of a story, you quickly tell the main things that happened. Here's the plot for the story about the three pigs: Three pigs built houses to protect them from the big bad wolf. The first pig built a house of straw, but the wolf huffed and puffed and blew the house down. The second pig built a house of wood, but the wolf huffed and puffed and blew the house down. The third pig built a house of brick. The wolf huffed and puffed but could not blow the house down.

5. Your turn: Tell me the plot for the story about the velveteen rabbit. Quickly tell the important things that happened in the story. (Call on a student. Accept reasonable responses.)

6. Everybody, find part D on your worksheet. ✔
   • You're going to answer questions about the setting, the characters, and the plot for *The Velveteen Rabbit*.
   • Item 1 on your worksheet asks: What is the setting for the beginning of the story? Write the answer to item 1. Raise your hand when you've done that much.
     (Observe students and give feedback.)
   • What's the answer to item 1? (Call on a student. Idea: *Timmy's house.*)

7. Item 2 says: Name the two main characters in this story. There are two main characters in this story and some other characters that are not main characters. The main characters are the ones who do things that are important.
   • Write the answer to item 2. Raise your hand when you've done that much.
     (Observe students and give feedback.)
   • What's the answer to item 2? (Call on a student. Idea: *Timmy and the velveteen rabbit.*)

8. Item 3 asks: Which passage tells the plot for this story? There are three short passages— A, B, and C. Read each passage. Raise your hand when you know whether passage A, passage B, or passage C tells the plot.
   • (Teacher reference:)

   > a. A boy named Timmy got sick. A princess told Timmy that his velveteen rabbit would help him get well. When Timmy was older, his mother put the rabbit in the woods. She thought Timmy was too big to have a toy rabbit.
   > b. Timmy's favorite toy was a stuffed velveteen rabbit. A princess told him it was real. Timmy's mother didn't like the toy rabbit, so she bought Timmy a real rabbit. Timmy liked the real rabbit so much that he forgot all about his old stuffed toy.
   > c. Timmy's favorite toy was a stuffed velveteen rabbit. Timmy believed the rabbit was real. When Timmy got sick, the rabbit helped him get better. When Timmy was older, he left the rabbit in the woods. When he looked back, there was a live rabbit right where he had left his toy.

   • Read the passage that tells the plot. (Call on a student. Student should read passage C.)
   • Everybody, write **C** as the answer to item 3. ✔

Activities

1. (Direct students to write about their favorite "soft-and-cuddly." They are to tell when they got it and why they liked it better than any other stuffed animal they had.)
2. (After students have completed their accounts, have students read them to the class.)
3. (Direct students to draw a picture of their soft-and-cuddly or bring it to class if they still have it.)
4. (Post stories and pictures.)

A **Literature Lesson 1** *The Velveteen Rabbit*

1
1. cuddly
2. receive
3. shabby
4. princess

2
1. search
2. snuggle
3. tattered
4. velveteen

3
1. searched
2. received
3. snuggled
4. remembered
5. stuffing

4
1. shabbier
2. birthday
3. Timmy
4. bunny
5. bunnies
6. months

B **Write answers to these questions on lined paper.**

1. How old was Timmy when he got the velveteen rabbit?

2. What color was the rabbit?

3. What did the rabbit look like after Timmy had it a few years?

4. Who thought that Timmy should get rid of the velveteen rabbit?

5. In Timmy's dream, who told him something about his rabbit?

6. What did that person say would happen to the rabbit?

7. Where did his mother tell him to take the tattered rabbit?

8. When Timmy looked back at the rabbit, how had it changed?

All stories have three main elements. They are the **setting,** the **characters** and the **plot.**
- The **setting** is where and when the story takes place.
- The **characters** are the important people, animals or objects that do things in the story.
- The **plot** is what happens to the characters in the story.

D Answer these questions about the story *The Velveteen Rabbit.*

1. What is the setting for the beginning of the story?

_____

2. Name the two main characters in this story.

_____

3. Which passage tells the plot for this story?

_____

a. A boy named Timmy got sick. A princess told Timmy that his velveteen rabbit would help him get well. When Timmy was older, his mother put the rabbit in the woods. She thought Timmy was too big to have a toy rabbit.

b. Timmy's favorite toy was a stuffed velveteen rabbit. A princess told him it was real. Timmy's mother didn't like the toy rabbit, so she bought Timmy a real rabbit. Timmy liked the real rabbit so much that he forgot all about his old stuffed toy.

c. Timmy's favorite toy was a stuffed velveteen rabbit. Timmy believed the rabbit was real. When Timmy got sick, the rabbit helped him get better. When Timmy was older, he left the rabbit in the woods. When he looked back, there was a live rabbit right where he had left his toy.

Literature Lesson 2

2-1 *Dreams*

Written by Langston Hughes

Illustrated by Anni Matsick

Theme: Dream metaphors

Dreams is a poem that tells why a person should hold on to dreams.

2-2 *The Runner*

Written by Faustin Charles

Illustrated by Kate Flanagan

Theme: Fantastic ability

The Runner is a poem that compares the speed of a running man to the speed of other things.

Materials Needed for Lesson 2-1

> 1 copy of the literature anthology for each student
> 1 copy of blackline master 2A for each student
> Writing materials
> Drawing materials

Materials Needed for Lesson 2-2

> 1 copy of the literature anthology for each student
> Drawing materials

Presenting Lesson 2–1

1. Find page 17 in your anthology. ✔
- I'll read this poem to you. Then we'll go over what it means. Listen to the whole poem.
- (Read the whole poem.)
- (Teacher reference:)

> ### Dreams
> Hold fast to dreams
> For if dreams die
> Life is a broken-winged bird
> That cannot fly.
>
> Hold fast to dreams
> For when dreams go
> Life is a barren field
> Frozen with snow.

2. Here's the first part of the poem:

> Hold fast to dreams
> For if dreams die
> Life is a broken-winged bird
> That cannot fly.

- Everybody, can a bird with a broken wing fly? (Signal.) *No.*
- When you **hold fast** to something, you don't let it go.
- The poem says that if dreams die, life is a broken-winged bird that cannot fly. In what ways would life without dreams be like a broken-winged bird? (Call on a student. Idea: *Without purpose.*)

3. Here's the next part:

> Hold fast to dreams
> For when dreams go
> Life is a barren field
> Frozen with snow.

- That part starts like the first part. What does **hold fast** mean? (Call on a student. Idea: *Don't let go.*)
- That part says that without dreams life is a barren field frozen with snow. A barren field is a bare field. In what ways would life without dreams be like a barren field with snow? (Call on a student. Ideas: *Cold, without color.*)
- Everybody, does the writer think life without dreams is **happy** or **sad?** (Signal.) *Sad.*
- How do you know? (Call on a student. Idea: *Because the writer says life without dreams is like a broken-winged bird and a frozen field of snow.*)

4. Raise your hand if you'd like to read part of the poem.
(Call on individual students, each to read one of the stanzas.)

Literature Types

1. (Make copies of blackline master 2A.)

2. (Distribute copies of blackline master 2A to students.)

3. Find part A on your worksheet. ✔

- Follow along as I read. There are different types of literature. Some literature is **fiction.** This is material that is made up and did not really happen. Fiction is false. The other type of literature is non-fiction. Non-fiction literature is true. It tells about real people or things.

4. Everybody, what do we call literature that is false? (Signal.) *Fiction.*

- What do we call literature that is true? (Signal.) *Nonfiction.*

5. There are different kinds of fiction. Whether the literature is true or not, it can be presented in many forms. Those forms are stories; drama (or plays); and poetry. Who can name three ways that literature can be presented? (Call on a student. Idea: *Stories, plays, poetry.*)

- Remember, fiction is false. Non-fiction is true. And there are different ways of presenting either fiction or non-fiction—as stories, as plays, and as poetry.

6. (Tell the students when they should complete the items in part B.)

7. (After the students complete the items, do a workcheck. For each item: Read the item. Call on a student to say the answer. If the answer is wrong, say the correct answer.)

Answer Key: **1.** non-fiction   **2.** fiction   **3.** stories, drama (or plays), poetry

Activities

1. Find part C on your worksheet. ✔

• (Direct students to make up another part for the poem, starting with "Hold fast to dreams," and giving other reasons why.)

2. (Direct students to draw pictures of dreams they have or that they like to remember.)

Presenting Lesson 2-2

1. Find page 18 in your anthology. ✔

• Here's the title of the next poem we'll read: The Runner.
  Everybody, what's the title? (Signal.) *The Runner.*

2. I'll read the whole poem twice. Listen for the names of things that are not as fast as the runner. See how many of them you can remember. You may want to write down the names of some of the things.

• (Read the poem two times.)

• (Teacher reference:)

The Runner

Run, run, runner man,
As fast as you can,
Faster than the speed of light,
Smoother than a bird in flight.
Run, run, runner man,
No one can catch the runner man,
Swifter than an arrow,
Outrunning his own shadow.
Run, run, runner man,
Faster than tomorrow.
Run, run, runner man,
Quicker than a rocket!
Into deep space spinning a comet!
Run, run, runner man,
Lighting the heavens of the night,
Run, run, runner man,
Out of sight,
Run, run, runner man, run!

• Everybody, could a person really run as fast as the man in the poem? (Signal.) *No.*

• Name some of the things that are not as fast as the runner in the poem. (Call on individual students. Ideas: *Speed of light, other people, an arrow, his shadow, a rocket.*)

- If the poem is not about a real person, what do you think it's about? (Call on individual students. Ideas: *How it feels to run fast; a dream about running; an imaginary runner.*)
- How do you feel when you're running fast? (Call on individual students.)
3. Raise your hand if you'd like to read part of this poem. (Call on individual students to read parts of the poem.)

Activity

- (Direct students to draw a picture about running fast.)

Literature Lesson 2

There are different types of literature. Some literature is **fiction.** This is material that is made up and did not really happen. Fiction is false.

The other type of literature is **non-fiction.** Non-fiction literature is true. It tells about real people or things.

There are different kinds of fiction. Whether the literature is true or not, it can be presented in many forms. Those forms are stories; drama or plays; and poetry.

B Answer these questions.

1. What do we call literature that is true? _____

2. What do we call literature that is false? _____

3. Name the **3** main ways that literature is presented. _____

_____

C Make up another part for the poem.

Hold fast to dreams

_____

_____

_____

_____

_____

_____

The Emperor's New Clothes

Adapted by Harvey Cleaver

Illustrated by Jenny Williams

Theme: Admitting the truth

The Emperor's New Clothes is the tale of a vain king who is tricked into wearing clothes that don't exist.

Materials Needed for Lesson

1 copy of the literature anthology for each student
1 copy of blackline masters 3A, 3B, and 3C for each student
1 copy of blackline master 3D for each group of 4 students
Lined paper

Presenting the Lesson

1. (Make copies of blackline masters.)
2. (Distribute copies of blackline masters 3A, 3B, and 3C to students. Direct students to read orally the words in columns 1 and 2 of part A. Explain what the words mean.)
- (Teacher reference:)

1	2
1. deafening	1. magnificent
2. admit	2. splendid
3. emperor	3. flattering
4. carriage	4. tailor
5. fabric	

- Very loud sounds are called **deafening.** If you are close to a deafening sound for a long time, you become deaf for a few minutes.
- When you **admit** that something is true, you say that it is true.
- An **emperor** is like a king who rules a country.
- A **carriage** is a vehicle that has doors and windows and that is pulled by horses.
- **Fabric** is cloth.
- Things that are **magnificent** are very beautiful.

- **Splendid** is another word for magnificent. A splendid house is a magnificent house.
- Things that **flatter** somebody tell how good or smart the person is. Here are some flattering statements: "You are so good looking; My, how smart you are; Aren't you the most clever person I've ever seen." Sometimes flattering statements sound true even if they're not true.
- A **tailor** is a person who makes clothing.
3. (Direct students to read orally the words in columns 3 through 6.)
- (Teacher reference:)

3	4	5	6
1. busiest	1. puzzled	1. wherever	1. embarrass
2. differently	2. reminded	2. clever	2. embarrassment
3. wisest	3. swelled	3. route	3. invisible
4. exciting	4. hearted	4. indeed	4. jacket
5. actually	5. naked	5. clothing	5. instant
	6. neared	6. parade	6. jealous

4. (Direct students to read the story aloud, calling on individual students to read two or three sentences at a time. Tell students to raise their hand and ask a question about anything in the story that they don't understand.)
5. (After students have completed the story, direct them to write answers to the questions in part B of blackline master 3A.)

(Answer Key:)
1. Why did the emperor's palace have so many mirrors?
   Idea: *Because he loved to look at himself in his fine clothes.*
2. How many tailors spent all their time making clothes for the emperor? *3.*
3. The thief told the emperor that only the _____ people would be able to see the magic fabric he had. Ideas: *Wisest, smartest.*
4. Why didn't the emperor admit that he could not see the magic fabric?
   Idea: *Because he didn't want to look like a fool.*
5. How much did the emperor pay for his new suit of clothes? *20 gold coins.*
6. Why didn't the queen say that the king was naked?
   Idea: *Because she didn't want to look like a fool.*
7. Why did the emperor have a parade? Idea: *To show off his new clothes.*
8. Who finally asked why the emperor was naked? Idea: *A child.*
9. What did the crowd do when people realized that the emperor was naked?
   Idea: *Laughed.*
10. How did the emperor change after that day?
    Ideas: *He was wiser; he didn't care as much about clothes.*

Retelling the Story

1. I'm going to call on individual students to retell different parts of this story. Who wants to start with the title and tell the first part of the story? (Call on a student. After the student has told the first part of the story, call on another student to start there and tell more of the story. Continue until the story has been retold. Praise accounts that present the important details of the story.)

2. (Repeat the procedure, calling on individual students.)

Optional—New Ending

- Raise your hand if you can tell the story with a different ending. (Call on a student.) Start where the thief brings the emperor a new suit and tell the new ending.

Optional—Dramatization

- What part of the story do you like the best? (Call on individual students.)
- (Select one of the scenes.) Let's act out that part. (Assign students to play the roles of the characters and act out the selected scene.)

Literary Elements

1. Find part C on your worksheet. ✔
- You're going to answer questions about the setting, the characters, and the plot for the story *The Emperor's New Clothes.*

2. Item 1 asks: What is the main setting for this story? Everybody, write the answer to item 1. Raise your hand when you've done that much.
   (Observe students and give feedback.)
- What's the answer to item 1? (Call on a student. Idea: *The palace.*)

3. Item 2 says: Name the main character in this story. Everybody, write the answer to item 2. Raise your hand when you've done that much.
   (Observe students and give feedback.)
- Everybody, what's the answer to item 2? (Signal.) *The Emperor.*

4. Item 3 asks: Which passage tells the plot for this story? There are three short passages— A, B, and C. Read each passage. Raise your hand when you know whether passage A, passage B, or passage C tells the plot.
- (Teacher reference:)

   a. A thief sold a new suit to the Emperor, a suit that no one could see. The thief said that only smart people could see the suit. Nobody wanted to look stupid, so everyone pretended they could see the suit. The Emperor paraded through the town completely naked. A child asked, "Why is the Emperor naked?" Then everyone knew they had been fooled.

   b. A thief sold a new suit to the Emperor, a suit that no one could see. The thief said only smart people could see the suit. The Emperor's wife was one of the smartest people the Emperor knew. He asked her if she could see the new suit. She was not afraid of looking stupid, so she said, "No, I cannot see it. You are completely naked!" The Emperor laughed and ordered his guards to take the thief to jail.

c. The Emperor ordered a new suit for himself, a suit that no one could see. When he wore the suit, the Emperor became invisible. No one could see him when he walked through the town. One night, a thief stole the suit while the Emperor was sleeping. After that, the thief was able to steal many things from the people of the town because no one could see him.

- Read the passage that tells the plot. (Call on a student. Student should read passage A.)
- Everybody, write **A** as the answer to item 3. ✔

Literature Types

1. Find part D on your worksheet. ✔
- You learned about the types of literature. Everybody, what do we call literature that is false? (Signal.) *Fiction.*
- What do we call literature that is true? (Signal.) *Non-fiction.*
2. Literature can be presented in three main forms. What are those forms? (Call on individual students. Idea: *Stories, plays, poems.*)
- Remember, fiction is false. Non-fiction is true. There are different ways of presenting either fiction or non-fiction—as stories, as plays, and as poetry.
3. (Tell students when they should complete the items.)
4. (After the students complete the items, do a workcheck. For each item: Read the item. Call on a student to say the answer. If the answer is wrong, say the correct answer.)

Answer Key: **1.** fiction   **2.** non-fiction   **3.** Idea: Stories, plays, and poetry

Author's Purpose

1. Find part E on your worksheet. ✔
- These are titles of articles. You can tell by the title what the author's purpose is. The first word above the list of titles is **persuade.** Touch that word. ✔
- For some articles, the author is trying to persuade the reader to think a particular way. An article that persuades may try to convince you that you should go barefoot all the time or do something else that you normally wouldn't do or wouldn't think.
2. The next word above the list of titles is **entertain.** The purpose of these articles is to tell you things that are interesting or funny.
3. The third word above the titles is **inform.** When an author tries to inform, the author gives information and facts that you may not know. Some articles that inform tell you how to make things or do things that you don't already know. Some give you information about places that you might want to visit or information about things that happened a long time ago. Remember, if it tells about things that you probably don't know, the author is trying to inform you.

4. Everybody, if an article is very funny, what is the author's purpose? (Signal.) *To entertain.*

- If an article tries to talk you into changing your mind about something, what is the author's purpose? (Signal.) *To persuade.*

- If the author tells you about things you never knew, what is the author's purpose? (Signal.) *To inform.*

- (Repeat step 4 until firm.)

5. Title 1: How to Care for Wild Birds.
Everybody, what's the author's purpose? (Signal.) *To inform.*

6. Title 2: Don't Vote for Sherman Brown. What's the author's purpose? (Signal.) *To persuade.*

7. Title 3: Molly's Magic Marble. What's the author's purpose? (Signal.) *To entertain.*

8. Title 4: Easy Bread Recipes. What's the author's purpose? (Signal.) *To inform.*

9. (Tell the students when they should complete the items.)

10. (After the students complete the items, do a workcheck. For each item: Read the item. Call on a student to say the answer. If the answer is wrong, say the correct answer.)

Answer Key: **1.** inform   **2.** persuade   **3.** entertain   **4.** inform   **5.** entertain
 6. persuade   **7.** inform   **8.** inform   **9.** persuade   **10.** entertain

Activities

1. (Assign students to groups of 4 or 5. Distribute copies of blackline master 3D to each group.)

- (Tell students:) You're going to write a story about the emperor after he had changed. I'll read the first part of the story.

> Two years after the parade, a thief came to the emperor's palace. The thief pretended to be a tailor. The thief told the emperor that he had a magnificent fabric that appeared to be invisible to fools.

- You're going to finish this story. You'll tell what the emperor said and what he did to the thief.

2. (After students have written their story, have a student from each group read their group's story to the class.)

3. (Students may want to put on a play that incorporates the best of what the different stories presented.)

Ⓐ Literature Lesson 3 *The Emperor's New Clothes*

1
1. deafening
2. admit
3. emperor
4. carriage
5. fabric

2
1. magnificent
2. splendid
3. flattering
4. tailor

3
1. busiest
2. differently
3. wisest
4. exciting
5. actually

4
1. puzzled
2. reminded
3. swelled
4. hearted
5. naked
6. neared

5
1. wherever
2. clever
3. route
4. indeed
5. clothing
6. parade

6
1. embarrass
2. embarrassment
3. invisible
4. jacket
5. instant
6. jealous

Ⓑ Write answers to these questions on lined paper.

1. Why did the emperor's palace have so many mirrors?

2. How many tailors spent all their time making clothes for the emperor?

3. The thief told the emperor that only the ▮▮▮▮▮▮ people would be able to see the magic fabric he had.

4. Why didn't the emperor admit that he could not see the magic fabric?

5. How much did the emperor pay for his new suit of clothes?

6. Why didn't the queen say that the king was naked?

7. Why did the emperor have a parade?

8. Who finally asked why the emperor was naked?

9. What did the crowd do when people realized that the emperor was naked?

10. How did the emperor change after that day?

C **Answer these questions about the story *The Emperor's New Clothes.***

1. What is the main setting for this story? _____

2. Name the main character in this story. _____

3. Which passage tells the plot for this story? _____

    a. A thief sold a new suit to the Emperor, a suit that no one could see. The thief said that only smart people could see the suit. Nobody wanted to look stupid, so everyone pretended they could see the suit. The Emperor paraded through the town completely naked. A child asked, "Why is the Emperor naked?" Then everyone knew they had been fooled.

    b. A thief sold a new suit to the Emperor, a suit that no one could see. The thief said only smart people could see the suit. The Emperor's wife was one of the smartest people the Emperor knew. He asked her if she could see the new suit. She was not afraid of looking stupid, so she said, "No, I cannot see it. You are completely naked!" The Emperor laughed and ordered his guards to take the thief to jail.

    c. The Emperor ordered a new suit for himself, a suit that no one could see. When he wore the suit, the Emperor became invisible. No one could see him when he walked through the town. One night, a thief stole the suit while the Emperor was sleeping. After that, the thief was able to steal many things from the people of the town because no one could see him.

D **Answer these questions.**

1. What do we call literature that is false? _____

2. What do we call literature that is true? _____

3. Name the 3 main ways that literature is presented. _____

_____

E **Write the author's purpose for each item.**

persuade   entertain   inform

1. How to Care for Wild Birds _____

2. Don't Vote for Sherman Brown _____

3. Molly's Magic Marble _____

4. Easy Bread Recipes _____

5. Melvyn Goes to Mars _____

6. Why You Need a New Car _____

7. Growing Vegetables Indoors _____

8. How to Build a Tree House _____

9. 10 Reasons for Not Eating Junk _____

10. Attack of the Undersea Brains _____

Literature Lesson 3 *The Emperor's New Clothes*
Finish the story.

Two years after the parade, a thief came to the Emperor's palace. The thief pretended to be a tailor. The thief told the Emperor that he had a magnificent fabric that appeared to be invisible to fools.

_____

_____

_____

_____

_____

_____

_____

_____

_____

_____

_____

_____

_____

Literature Lesson 4

To be presented with Lesson 40
Anthology page 35

Why Leopard Has Black Spots

Written by Won-Ldy Paye

Edited by Margaret H. Lippert

Illustrated by Ted Eink

Theme: Deceit

Why Leopard Has Black Spots is an African fable that teaches that a liar usually gets caught and pays a penalty.

Materials Needed for Lesson

1 copy of the literature anthology for each student
1 copy of blackline masters 4A, 4B, 4C, and 4D for each student
Lined paper
Drawing materials

Materials for Optional Activities
Computer, encyclopedia, or other research resources

Presenting the Lesson

1. (Make copies of blackline masters.)
2. (Distribute copies of blackline masters 4A, 4B, and 4C to students. Direct students to read orally the words in column 1 of part A. Explain what the words mean.)
- (Teacher reference:)

1
1. cucumber
2. provide
3. invite
4. leopard
5. entrance

- A **cucumber** is a vegetable that is shaped like a pickle. In fact, pickles are made from small cucumbers.
- **Provide** is another word for **give.** When you provide help, you give help.
- When you **invite** people to do something, you politely ask them to do it. Would you like to come **to my party?**

- A **leopard** is a member of the cat family that has spots and lives in Africa.
- The **entrance** to a place is where you go into the place.

3. (Direct students to read orally the words in column 2.)
- (Teacher reference:)

2
1. vegetables
2. honest
3. tomatoes
4. cover
5. single

4. (Direct students to read the story aloud, calling on individual students to read two or three sentences at a time. Tell students to raise their hand and ask a question about anything in the story that they don't understand.)
5. (After students have completed the story, direct them to write answers to the questions in part B of blackline master 4A.)

(Answer Key:)
1. At the beginning of this story, what was unusual about how the leopard looked?
   Idea: *It had no spots.*
2. Who had a garden?
   Spider.
3. What kept happening to the things in the garden?
   Idea: *They would disappear.*
4. Which animals did Spider ask about the missing vegetables?
   Deer and Leopard.
5. Who had a plan to find out who was taking the vegetables?
   Deer.
6. Who really took things from the garden?
   Deer.
7. How did Deer trick Leopard into going to the garden?
   Idea: *Deer told Leopard that Spider called him.*
8. What happened to Leopard when he got there?
   Idea: *He fell into a hole with red-hot coals.*
9. How did that change Leopard?
   Idea: *He got black spots on his skin.*
10. From that day on, which two animals were great enemies?
    Deer and Leopard.

Retelling the Story

1. I'm going to call on individual students to retell different parts of this story. Who wants to start with the title and tell the first part of the story? (Call on a student. After the student has told the first part of the story, call on another student to start there and tell more of the story. Continue until the story has been retold. Praise accounts that present the important details of the story.)
2. (Repeat the procedure, calling on individual students.)

Optional—New Ending

- Raise your hand if you can tell the story with a different ending. (Call on a student.) Start where Deer tells Spider about building a fire pit and tell the new ending.

Optional—Dramatization

- What part of the story do you like the best? (Call on individual students.)
- (Select one of the scenes.) Let's act out that part. (Assign students to play the roles of the characters and act out the selected scene.)

Literary Elements

1. Find part C on your worksheet. ✔
- You're going to answer questions about the setting, the characters, and the plot for the story *Why Leopard Has Black Spots.*
2. Item 1 asks: What is the main setting for this story? Is the main setting a city, a village, or on the ocean? Write the answer to item 1. Raise your hand when you've done that much.

   (Observe students and give feedback.)
- Everybody, what's the answer to item 1? (Signal.) *A village.*
3. Item 2 says: Name the 3 main characters in this story. Everybody, write the answer to item 2. Raise your hand when you've done that much.

   (Observe students and give feedback.)
- What's the answer to item 2? (Call on a student.) *Deer, Spider, and Leopard.*
4. Item 3 asks: Which passage tells the plot for this story? Read each passage. Raise your hand when you know whether passage A, passage B, or passage C tells the plot.

- (Teacher reference:)

> a. Deer, Leopard and Spider ate dinner together every night at Spider's house. Spider had a big garden, but a thief was stealing some of the vegetables. One night, Deer, Leopard and Spider set a trap for the thief. They waited all night, but the thief didn't come. Leopard was so tired, he forgot where the trap was and fell into it by accident. A fire in the trap made black spots all over Leopard.
>
> b. Someone was taking vegetables from Spider's garden. Deer said it wasn't him. Leopard said it wasn't him, either, but the vegetables kept disappearing from Spider's garden. Deer told Spider how to set a trap for the thief. Then, Deer led Leopard into the trap. First, Spider believed Leopard was really the thief. Then, Spider and Leopard realized it had to be Deer. A fire in the trap made black spots all over Leopard.
>
> c. Deer, Leopard and Spider ate dinner together every night at Spider's house. Spider had a big garden, but a thief was stealing some of the vegetables. Deer told Spider how to set a trap for the thief. The next night, Deer tripped over a log and fell into the trap. A fire in the trap made black spots all over Deer.

- Read the passage that tells the plot. (Call on a student. Student should read passage B.)
- Everybody, write B as the answer to item 3. ✔

Fables

1. Find part D on your worksheet. ✔
- Follow along while I read. One type of literature is a fable. A fable is fiction, but it is a special kind of fiction. It gives the reader a lesson or a message.
2. You just read the fable about a leopard. The lesson of the fable is **Things aren't always what they seem to be.**
- Everybody, say that lesson. Get ready. (Signal.) *Things aren't always what they seem to be.*
- Why did it seem like Leopard was the thief? (Call on a student. Idea: *Because he got caught in the trap.*)
- Who was really the thief? (Call on a student. Idea: *The deer.*)
- How did Spider find out that Deer was the thief? (Call on a student. Idea: *He found out that Deer had tricked Leopard into getting trapped.*)
3. (Tell students when they should do the items in part D.)
4. (After the students complete the items, do a workcheck. For each item: Read the item. Call on a student to say the answer. If the answer is wrong, say the correct answer.)

Answer Key: **1.** Idea: Things aren't always what they seem to be. **2.** Idea: Because he got caught in the trap. **3.** Deer

Activities
Parables

1. (After students have read *Why Leopard Has Black Spots,* discuss how Leopard got those spots in the story.)

2. (Direct groups to make up stories about a zebra or another animal. Explain:)

> A zebra has stripes. Make up a story that tells how that happened. First figure out what could make such marks. Could something that scratches make those marks?
>
> Could something that stains make those marks?
>
> Could something that burns make those marks?
>
> After you figure out some way that the marks could be made, make up a story that tells how the zebra got in a situation that gave her those marks.
>
> Don't make your story like the one about the leopard.

- (Discuss possibilities with the whole class. Then have groups of about 4 write and illustrate their story. Groups may share their stories with the class or with another class.)

Camouflage

3. (Pass out blackline master 4D. Tell students:)

> Picture 1 shows a white horse in a field next to some trees. The sun is making long shadows, but only one shadow is shown. That shadow is going up and over the horse. Make shadows for the other trees. Each shadow goes across the ground and up and over the animal. When you are done, you will have an animal that can hide very well in the shadows of trees.

- (Discuss what animal the picture shows and why this sort of camouflage could serve zebras well when they are resting on the plain. It also may give a clue about where they would like to rest.)

4. (Use a similar procedure for picture 2. Explain:)

> Picture 2 shows a big cat. Above the cat is a branch with many leaves. Each leaf is going to make a shadow. The dotted lines show where the shadows will be formed on the cat. The shadow for one leaf is already shown. Make shadows for the other leaves.

- (Discuss what animal the picture shows and why this sort of camouflage would serve leopards well. It also shows where they like to hide.)

- (Teacher reference: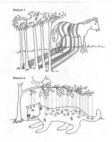

Optional Activities

- (Groups that are interested in how other animals camouflage themselves may pick an animal and do some library or computer research to find good pictures of the animal camouflaged. Each group may then make a presentation to the class.)

A **Literature Lesson 4** *Why Leopard Has Black Spots*

1
1. cucumber
2. provide
3. invite
4. leopard
5. entrance

2
1. vegetables
2. honest
3. tomatoes
4. cover
5. single

B **Write answers to these questions on lined paper.**

1. At the beginning of this story, what was unusual about how the leopard looked?

2. Who had a garden?

3. What kept happening to the things in the garden?

4. Which animals did Spider ask about the missing vegetables?

5. Who had a plan to find out who was taking the vegetables?

6. Who really took things from the garden?

7. How did Deer trick Leopard into going to the garden?

8. What happened to Leopard when he got there?

9. How did that change Leopard?

10. From that day on, which two animals were great enemies?

Ⓒ Answer these questions about the story *Why Leopard Has Black Spots.*

1. What is the main setting for this story? _____

_____

2. Name the 3 main characters in this story. _____

_____

3. Which passage tells the plot for this story? _____

a. Deer, Leopard and Spider ate dinner together every night at Spider's house. Spider had a big garden, but a thief was stealing some of the vegetables. One night, Deer, Leopard and Spider set a trap for the thief. They waited all night, but the thief didn't come. Leopard was so tired, he forgot where the trap was and fell into it by accident. A fire in the trap made black spots all over Leopard.

b. Someone was taking vegetables from Spider's garden. Deer said it wasn't him. Leopard said it wasn't him, either, but the vegetables kept disappearing from Spider's garden. Deer told Spider how to set a trap for the thief. Then, Deer led Leopard into the trap. First, Spider believed Leopard was really the thief. Then, Spider and Leopard realized it had to be Deer. A fire in the trap made black spots all over Leopard.

c. Deer, Leopard and Spider ate dinner together every night at Spider's house. Spider had a big garden, but a thief was stealing some of the vegetables. Deer told Spider how to set a trap for the thief. The next night, Deer tripped over a log and fell into the trap. A fire in the trap made black spots all over Deer.

One type of literature is a **fable.** A **fable** is fiction, but it is a special kind of fiction. It gives the reader a lesson or a message.

1. You read a fable about a leopard. What was the lesson of that fable? _____

_____

2. Why did it seem like Leopard was the thief? _____

_____

_____

3. Who was really the thief? _____

Picture 1

Picture 2

Literature Lesson 5

Lesson 5-1 to be presented with Lesson 50
Anthology page 45

Lesson 5-2 can be presented at a later time.

5-1 *Boar Out There*

Written by Cynthia Rylant

Illustrated by Fred Marvin

Theme: Fear

Boar Out There tells how a young girl is afraid of and yet fascinated by a wild boar that lives in the woods near her home.

5-2 "Crossing the Creek"

(from *Little House on the Prairie*)

Written by Laura Ingalls Wilder

Illustrated by Garth Williams

Theme: Fear

"Crossing the Creek" is the first of two chapters that tell about a pioneer family's trip across the prairie.

Materials Needed for Lesson 5-1

1 copy of the literature anthology for each student
1 copy of blackline masters 5A and 5B for each student
Drawing materials
Lined paper

Materials Needed for Read-to Lesson 5-2

1 copy of blackline master 5C for each student

Presenting Lesson 5-1

1. (Make copies of blackline masters 5A and 5B.)

2. (Distribute copies of blackline masters 5A and 5B to students. Direct students to read orally the words in columns 1 and 2. Explain what the words mean.)

- (Teacher reference:)

1
1. ragged
2. boar
3. bristles
4. bristling
5. nostrils
6. teaberry
7. twirl
8. terror

2
1. rigid
2. linger
3. glide
4. briar
5. astonishing
6. glistened
7. bluejay
8. absolutely

- **Ragged** is another word for **torn** or **ripped.** A ragged coat is a torn coat.
- A **boar** is a wild pig with large tusks that are powerful weapons.
- **Bristles** are stiff hairs. Brushes have bristles. Boars have bristles.
- When animals are **bristling** their bristles stand up.
- Your **nostrils** are the two holes in your nose.
- **Teaberry** is a plant that has minty tasting leaves.
- **Twirl** means **spin** or **twist.** When something spins around, it is twirling.
- **Terror** is another word for **great fear.** If he was in great fear, he was in terror.
- **Rigid** is another word for **stiff.** A board that is stiff and firm is rigid.
- Something that goes away very slowly **lingers.** The flavor of gum lingers in your mouth.
- When birds **glide,** they float through the air without moving their wings.
- A **briar** is a prickly shrub. Briar patches are so thick with briars that you couldn't walk through them.
- Something that is **astonishing** is **amazing** or **unbelievable.** An unbelievable trip is an astonishing trip.
- **Glistened** is another word for **shined** or **sparkled.** If the sun sparkled on the water, the sun glistened on the water.
- A **bluejay** is a blue bird with a tall crest on its head.
- **Absolutely** means **certainly** or **without a doubt.** Something that is absolutely correct is correct without a doubt.

3. (Direct students to read orally the words in column 3.)

- (Teacher reference:)

3
1. confusing
2. scarred
3. flung
4. splintery
5. blood

4. (Direct students to read *Boar Out There* aloud, calling on individual students to read two or three sentences at a time. Tell students to raise their hand and ask a question about anything in the story that they don't understand.)

5. (After students have completed the story, direct them to write answers to the questions in part B of blackline master 5A.)

(Answer Key:)
  1. Where were the people in Glen Morgan afraid to go?
     Idea: *The woods over by the Miller farm.*
  2. Why were they afraid?
     Idea: *There was a wild boar.*
  3. Who went into the woods?
     Jenny.
  4. How was the boar different from the way Jenny imagined him?
     Ideas: *She thought he might have a golden horn and have no fear, but he had no horn and was fearful.*
  5. What did she do while the boar was near her?
     Ideas: *Choked, coughed, stayed still and silent, looked at him, cried.*
  6. What scared the boar away?
     A bluejay.
  7. Why did Jenny feel sorry for the boar?
     Idea: *Because he has torn ears and no golden horn and lives in fear of bluejays and little girls.*

Retelling the Story

1. I'm going to call on individual students to retell different parts of this story. Who wants to start with the title and tell the first part of the story? (Call on a student. After the student has told the first part of the story, call on another student to start there and tell more of the story. Continue until the story has been retold. Praise accounts that present the important details of the story.)

2. (Repeat the procedure, calling on individual students.)

Optional—New Ending

• Raise your hand if you can tell the story with a different ending. (Call on a student.) Start where Jenny meets the boar in the woods and tell the new ending.

Optional—Dramatization

• What part of the story do you like the best? (Call on individual students.)
• (Select one of the scenes.) Let's act out that part. (Assign students to play the roles of the characters and act out the selected scene.)

Literary Elements

1. Find part C on your worksheet. ✔

- You're going to answer questions about the setting, the characters, and the plot for the story *Boar Out There.*

2. Item 1 asks: What is the main setting for this story? Everybody, write the answer to item 1. Raise your hand when you've done that much.
(Observe students and give feedback.)

- Everybody, what's the answer to item 1? (Call on a student. Idea: *The woods.*)

3. Item 2 says: Name the main character in this story. Everybody, write the answer to item 2. Raise your hand when you've done that much.
(Observe students and give feedback.)

- Everybody, what's the answer to item 2? (Signal.) *Jenny.*

4. Item 3 says: Write the plot for this story on your lined paper. Listen. When you write the plot, tell what everyone was afraid of. Tell what happened to Jenny in the woods. Tell how her feelings changed. Write the plot. Raise your hand when you've done that much.
(Observe students and give feedback.)

- (Call on individual students to read the plot. Praise accounts that provide the information that the item specifies.)

Author's Purpose

1. Find part D on your worksheet. ✔

- These are titles of articles. You can tell by the title what the author's purpose is. The words above the list of titles are **persuade, entertain,** and **inform.**

2. Everybody, if an article is very funny, what is the author's purpose? (Signal.) *To entertain.*

- If the author tells you about things you never knew, what is the author's purpose? (Signal.) *To inform.*

- If an article tries to talk you into changing your mind about something, what is the author's purpose? (Signal.) *To persuade.*

- (Repeat step 2 until firm.)

3. Title 1: Old Owl's Last Wish. Everybody, what's the author's purpose? (Signal.) *To entertain.*

4. Title 2: Making and Flying Kites. What's the author's purpose? (Signal.) *To inform.*

5. Title 3: Why the School Needs Your Help. What's the author's purpose? (Signal.) *To persuade.*

6. Title 4: Milo Mutt's Favorite Dog Stories. What's the author's purpose? (Signal.) *To entertain.*

7. (Tell the students when they should complete the items.)

8. (After the students complete the items, do a workcheck. For each item: Read the item. Call on a student to say the answer. If the answer is wrong, say the correct answer.)

Answer Key: **1.** entertain **2.** inform **3.** persuade **4.** entertain **5.** entertain **6.** persuade **7.** persuade **8.** persuade **9.** inform **10.** inform

Activities

Maps

1. (After students read *Boar Out There,* discuss the physical arrangement of things the story names. Present items such as:)

- If Jenny went outside the fence on her way to the woods, name the object she would pass.
- Where was Jenny when she came in contact with the boar—on the edge of the woods or farther inside the woods?

2. (Direct groups of about 4 to make a map to show where the story took place. Show the fence, the Dodge, and the woods. Make a dotted line to show where Jenny went. Make an **X** to show where she was when the boar ran past her.)

Fear

3. (Discuss fear with the students. Explain:)

In the story *Boar Out There,* different characters were afraid of different things. What was the boar afraid of? What was Jenny afraid of?

- (Direct students to write about one thing they used to fear greatly. Students are to tell what happened to make them less afraid.)

Optional Activity for Lesson 5-1

- (Direct students to write a different ending for the story *Boar Out There*. The ending is to begin right after the paragraph that ends with this sentence: He shivered and glistened and was absolutely silent.)

Presenting Read-to Lesson 5-2

1. (Make copies of blackline master 5C.)
2. (Direct students to listen as you read the next literature selection: "Crossing the Creek." Tell students to raise their hand and ask a question about anything in the story that they don't understand.)
3. (Read to the students: "Crossing the Creek." See pages 149–153 of this guide. **Note:** This is an excerpt from *Little House on the Prairie*. Be sure to read the introduction to the students. Read only "Crossing the Creek." Do not read the second excerpt, "Camp on the High Prairie," until lesson 6-1.)
4. (Distribute copies of blackline master 5C to students. Direct students to write answers to the questions.)

(Answer Key:)

1. What kind of vehicle did the family travel in?
   Covered wagon.
2. Where did the family come from?
   (Big Woods of) Wisconsin.
3. In which direction were they going?
   West.
4. What did Pa do to the wagon to prepare it for crossing the creek?
   Idea: *Tied down the wagon-cover.*
5. How was Jack supposed to get across the creek?
   Swim.
6. Who jumped into the water in the middle of the creek?
   Pa.
7. Who drove the wagon?
   Ma.
8. Who was missing when the family got to the other side?
   Jack.
9. What did they think must have happened to him?
   Drowned.
10. How many people did they see after they crossed the creek?
    None.

A Literature Lesson 5-1 *Boar Out There*

1
1. ragged
2. boar
3. bristles
4. bristling
5. nostrils
6. teaberry
7. twirl
8. terror

2
1. rigid
2. linger
3. glide
4. briar
5. astonishing
6. glistened
7. bluejay
8. absolutely

3
1. confusing
2. scarred
3. flung
4. splintery
5. blood

B Write answers to these questions on lined paper.

1. Where were the people in Glen Morgan afraid to go?

2. Why were they afraid?

3. Who went into the woods?

4. How was the boar different from the way Jenny imagined him?

5. What did she do while the boar was near her?

6. What scared the boar away?

7. Why did Jenny feel sorry for the boar?

C **Answer these questions about the story *Boar Out There*.**

1. What is the main setting for this story? _____

_____

2. Name the main character in this story. _____

_____

3. Write the plot for this story on your lined paper. Tell what everyone was afraid of. Tell what happened to Jenny in the woods. Tell how her feelings changed.

D **Write the author's purpose for each item.**

persuade   entertain   inform

1. Old Owl's Last Wish _____

2. Making and Flying Kites _____

3. Why the School Needs Your Help _____

4. Milo Mutt's Favorite Dog Stories _____

5. The Mystery of Gumdrop Valley _____

6. Eat More Oats! _____

7. Five Reasons to Grow Beans _____

8. What's Wrong With Chewing Gum? _____

9. Get Rid of Your Headaches _____

10. World's Fastest Cars _____

Literature Lesson 5-2 "Crossing the Creek"

1. What kind of vehicle did the family travel in?

_____

2. Where did the family come from?

_____

3. In which direction were they going?

_____

4. What did Pa do to the wagon to prepare it for crossing the creek?

_____

5. How was Jack supposed to get across the creek?

_____

6. Who jumped into the water in the middle of the creek?

_____

7. Who drove the wagon?

_____

8. Who was missing when the family got to the other side?

_____

9. What did they think must have happened to him?

_____

10. How many people did they see after they crossed the creek?

_____

Literature Lesson 6

Lesson 6-1 to be presented with Lesson 60

Lesson 6-2 can be presented at a later time. Anthology page 52

6-1 "Camp on the High Prairie"

(from *Little House on the Prairie*)

Written by Laura Ingalls Wilder

Illustrated by Garth Williams

Theme: Being safe

"Camp on the High Prairie" continues the story about a pioneer family's trip across the prairie.

6-2 *Spaghetti*

Written by Cynthia Rylant

Illustrated by Jim McGinnis

Theme: What makes life worthwhile

Spaghetti explains that everyone needs something special to love to make life worthwhile.

Materials Needed for Read-to Lesson 6-1

1 copy of blackline master 6A for each student

Materials Needed for Lesson 6-2

1 copy of the literature anthology for each student
1 copy of blackline masters 6B and 6C for each student
Lined paper

Optional: Drawing materials

Presenting Read-to Lesson 6-1

1. (Make copies of blackline master 6A.)
2. (Direct students to listen as you read "Camp on the High Prairie," the last excerpt from *Little House on the Prairie.* Tell students to raise their hand and ask a question about anything in the story that they do not understand.)
3. (Read to the students: "Camp on the High Prairie." See pages 153–156 of this guide.)
4. (Distribute copies of blackline master 6A to students. Direct students to write answers to the questions.)

(Answer Key:)
1. Why did Pa pull all the grass in a large circle?
   Idea: *He didn't want to take a chance of setting the prairie on fire.*
2. What did the horses do while Pa pulled the grass? Idea: *Rolled on the grass.*
3. Where did they get twigs for the fire? Idea: *From the creek bottoms.*
4. What did they eat for supper? Idea: *Cornmeal cakes, fried salt pork.*
5. What did they hear about a half mile away? *Wolf (wolves).*
6. What did Laura think she saw on the other side of the campfire? *A wolf.*
7. Why didn't Pa think she was right? Idea: *The horses weren't scared of it.*
8. Who walked toward the eyes? *Pa (or Charles).*
9. Who did the eyes belong to? *Jack.*
10. Why didn't Jack eat dinner? Idea: *He was too tired.*

Presenting Read-to Lesson 6-2

1. (Make copies of blackline masters 6B and 6C.)
2. (Distribute copies of blackline masters 6B and 6C to students. Direct students to read orally the words in columns 1 and 2 of part A. Explain what the words mean.)
- (Teacher reference:)

1	2
1. coyotes	1. hasty
2. glittering	2. dusk
3. erect	3. peering
4. stubborn	4. tingles
5. occurred	5. serious

- **Coyotes** are members of the dog and wolf family. They hunt in packs and howl at night.
- **Glittering** is another word for **glistening** or **sparkling.**
- When you **erect** something, you **build** it. If you erect a house, you build the house.
- People who are **stubborn** do not change their mind or give up doing what they want to do. A stubborn dog will keep doing something even though it gets punished.
- **Occurred** is another word for **happened.** Something that happened yesterday, occurred yesterday.

- **Hasty** is another word for **fast.** If you do things in a hasty way, you do them fast and maybe carelessly.
- **Dusk** is the time of day between sunset and complete darkness. At dusk, you can see things, but they are hard to see.
- **Peering** is another word for **staring.** When you are peering at something, you are staring at it.
- Something that **tingles** has a tickling feeling. Your mouth tingles when you are drinking a soft drink that bubbles.
- **Serious** is the opposite of **playful** or **funny.** If you are serious about doing something, you work hard at it. A serious story is one that is not funny.

3. (Direct students to read orally the words in columns 3 and 4.)
- (Teacher reference:)

3	4
1. crumbling	1. noodles
2. movie	2. faraway
3. Italian	3. spaghetti
4. theater	4. Gabriel
5. among	5. wobbling
6. pasta	

4. (Direct students to read *Spaghetti* aloud, calling on individual students to read two or three sentences at a time. Tell students to raise their hand and ask a question about anything in the story that they don't understand.)

5. (After students have completed the story, direct them to write answers to the questions in part B of blackline master 6B.)

(Answer Key:)
1. Where did Gabriel want to live at the beginning of the story? Idea: *Outside.*
2. Where did he actually live? Ideas: *In a tall building; in a city.*
3. What did he hear in the street? *A kitten (crying).*
4. What did Gabriel name the kitten? *Spaghetti.*
5. Why did he give it that name? Idea: *Because it smelled of pasta noodles.*
6. Who did Gabriel think owned the kitten? *(A friendly) Italian man.*
7. Where did Gabriel take the kitten at the end of the story?
   Ideas: *Inside; into his apartment; into his home.*
8. Why didn't Gabriel want to live with the coyotes now?
   Idea: *He has a pet (animal friend).*

Retelling the Story

1. I'm going to call on individual students to retell different parts of this story. Who wants to start with the title and tell the first part of the story? (Call on a student. After the student has told the first part of the story, call on another student to start there and tell more of the story. Continue until the story has been retold. Praise accounts that present the important details of the story.)

2. (Repeat the procedure, calling on individual students.)

Optional—New Ending

- Raise your hand if you can tell the story with a different ending. (Call on a student.) Start where Gabriel hears the kitten cry, and tell a new ending.

Literary Elements

1. Find part C on your worksheet. ✔
- You're going to answer questions about the setting, the characters, and the plot for the story *Spaghetti.*
2. Item 1 asks: What is the main setting for this story? Everybody, write the answer to item 1. Raise your hand when you've done that much.
(Observe students and give feedback.)
- What's the answer to item 1? (Call on a student. Ideas: *The city; Gabriel's neighborhood.*)
3. Item 2 says: Name the two main characters in this story. Write the answer to item 2. Raise your hand when you've done that much.
(Observe students and give feedback.)
- What's the answer to item 2? (Call on a student. Idea: *Gabriel and Spaghetti.*)
4. Item 3 says: Write the plot for this story. Tell about Gabriel. Tell how he felt before he found Spaghetti. Tell what happened to Gabriel. Tell how his feelings changed. Write the plot. Raise your hand when you've done that much.
(Observe students and give feedback.)
- (Call on individual students to read the plot. Praise accounts that provide the information that the item specifies.)

Activities for Lesson 6-2
Drawing inferences

1. (Discuss the changes in how Gabriel felt. Explain that Gabriel wanted to live in a tent before he found the kitten. Ask:)
Do you think he liked the place he lived in?
What happened that made him feel differently about where he lived?
How did he feel about where he lived at the end of the story?
Have you ever thought about living in a different kind of place than you live now?
2. (After students discuss these questions, direct students to write about the kind of place that they would like to live in. They may tell what it looks like and what they would like to do there. Or they may tell about the place they live in now and tell why they like it better than other places.)
- (Students may illustrate their descriptions.)

Literature Lesson 6-1 "Camp on the High Prairie"

1. Why did Pa pull all the grass in a large circle?

   _____

2. What did the horses do while Pa pulled the grass?

   _____

3. Where did they get twigs for the fire?

   _____

4. What did they eat for supper?

   _____

5. What did they hear about a half a mile away?

   _____

6. What did Laura think she saw on the other side of the campfire?

   _____

7. Why didn't Pa think she was right?

   _____

8. Who walked toward the eyes?

   _____

9. Who did the eyes belong to?

   _____

10. Why didn't Jack eat dinner?

   _____

A Literature Lesson   6-2 *Spaghetti*

1
1. coyotes
2. glittering
3. erect
4. stubborn
5. occurred

2
1. hasty
2. dusk
3. peering
4. tingles
5. serious

3
1. crumbling
2. movie
3. Italian
4. theater
5. among
6. pasta

4
1. noodles
2. faraway
3. spaghetti
4. Gabriel
5. wobbling

B Write answers to these questions on lined paper.

1. Where did Gabriel want to live at the beginning of the story?

2. Where did he actually live?

3. What did he hear in the street?

4. What did Gabriel name the kitten?

5. Why did he give it that name?

6. Who did Gabriel think owned the kitten?

7. Where did Gabriel take the kitten at the end of the story?

8. Why didn't Gabriel want to live with the coyotes now?

C **Answer these questions about the story *Spaghetti*.**

1. What is the main setting for this story?

   _____

2. Name the 2 main characters in this story.

   _____

3. Write the plot for this story. Tell about Gabriel. Tell how he felt before he found Spaghetti. Tell what happened to Gabriel. Tell how his feelings changed.

   _____

   _____

   _____

   _____

   _____

   _____

   _____

Literature Lesson 7

Charlie Best

Written by Ruth Corrin

Illustrated by Lesley Moyes

Theme: What's the evidence?

Charlie Best is about the importance of backing a story with evidence when nobody believes you're telling the truth.

Materials Needed for Lesson

1 copy of the literature anthology for each student
1 copy of blackline masters 7A and 7B for each student
1 copy of blackline master 7C for each group of 4 students
Lined paper
Drawing materials

Presenting the Lesson

1. (Make copies of blackline masters.)
2. (Distribute copies of blackline masters 7A and 7B to students. Direct students to read orally the words in columns 1 and 2 of part A. Explain what the words mean.)
- (Teacher reference:)

1
1. tidy
2. grope
3. nature
4. rumble
5. hitched

2
1. especially
2. bellowing
3. particularly
4. dreadful

- **Tidy** means **neat.** A neat house is a tidy house.
- When you **grope** for something, you try to find it. If you grope in the dark, you have to feel around with your hands.
- **Nature** refers to all things that are not made by humans. The birds, the sky, and the trees are all part of nature.
- When something **rumbles,** it makes a low growling sound.
- **Hitched up** means **hiked up** or **pulled up.** When you hitch up your pants, you pull them up at the waist.

- **Especially** means **most of all.** If he was especially interested in butterflies, he was interested in butterflies most of all.
- **Bellowing** is another word for yelling loudly.
- **Particularly** means **especially.** If something is particularly difficult, it is especially difficult.
- **Dreadful** is another word for **awful** or **horrible.** A dreadful experience is a horrible experience.

3. (Direct students to read orally the words in columns 3 through 5.)

- (Teacher reference:)

3
1. prickly
2. awfully
3. wonderfully
4. truly
5. wriggly
6. horribly
7. luckily

4
1. Charlie
2. Ms. Noble
3. schoolbag
4. whistle
5. tucked
6. emptied

5
1. scooped
2. dragon
3. slippery
4. untangled
5. sewing

4. (Direct students to read the story aloud, calling on individual students to read two or three sentences at a time. Tell students to raise their hand and ask a question about anything in the story that they don't understand.)

5. (After students have completed the story, direct them to write answers to the questions in part B of blackline master 7A.)

> (Answer Key:)
> 1. Why didn't Charlie get to school on time Monday morning?
>   Idea: *He climbed a mountain.*
> 2. What did he bring to school to prove that his story was true?
>   *Snow.*
> 3. What proof did he have that he tripped into a river?
>   *A (wriggly red) fish.*
> 4. What proof did he have that he went into a forest?
>   *A bird's nest (and mother bird).*
> 5. What proof did he have that he fell into a cave?
>   *A dragon.*
> 6. On which day was Charlie on time at school?
>   *Friday.*
> 7. Who made sure that he was on time?
>   *His dragon.*

Retelling the Story

1. I'm going to call on individual students to retell different parts of this story. Who wants to start with the title and tell the first part of the story? (Call on a student. After the student has told the first part of the story, call on another student to start there and tell more of the story. Continue until the story has been retold. Praise accounts that present the important details of the story.)
2. (Repeat the procedure, calling on individual students.)

Optional—New Ending

- Raise your hand if you can tell the story with a different ending. (Call on a student.) Start just before Charlie brings a dragon to class and tell the new ending.

Optional—Dramatization

- What part of the story do you like the best? (Call on individual students.)
- (Select one of the scenes.) Let's act out that part. (Assign students to play the roles of the characters and act out the selected scene.)

Literary Elements

1. Find part C on your worksheet. ✔
- You're going to answer questions about the setting, the characters, and the plot for the story *Charlie Best*.
2. Item 1 asks: What is the main setting for this story? Everybody, write the answer to item 1. Raise your hand when you've done that much.
(Observe students and give feedback.)
- What's the answer to item 1? (Call on a student. Idea: *A classroom.*)
3. Item 2 says: Name the two main characters in this story. Write the answer to item 2. Raise your hand when you've done that much. (Observe students and give feedback.)
- What's the answer to item 2? (Call on a student.) *Charlie Best and Ms. Noble.*
4. Item 3 says: Write the plot for this story. Tell about Charlie's problem and what he did. Tell about Ms. Noble. Tell about the surprise at the end of the story. Write the plot. Raise your hand when you're done. (Observe students and give feedback.)
- (Call on individual students to read the plot. Praise accounts that provide the information that the item specifies.)

Activities

Patterns of story grammar

1. (Discuss the pattern of events that occurs when Charlie comes to school late. Then direct groups of about 4 students to make up a new part to the story. The group is to write it so that Charlie is a mess. Then he tells a story that nobody could believe. But when it is finished, Charlie has something with him that he could not have unless his story were true.)

2. (Pass out blackline master 7C and direct students to follow along as you read:)
   Write your story so Ms. Noble says all the things she says at first. Then Charlie says all the things he says. Start the story this way:

   The next Thursday Charlie was late again.
   "What's the story?" said Ms. Noble.
   "Did you _____?"
   "Well, you see," said Charlie, "it's like this. . ."

- (Each group is to first discuss what happens to Charlie on his way to school and what evidence he brings with him. Then they are to complete the story on the blackline master.)

3. (After groups have finished their stories, they could illustrate them. They could also read their stories to the rest of the class.)

(Answer Key:)

Write your story so Ms. Noble says all the things she says at first. Then Charlie says all the things he says. Start the story this way:

The next Thursday Charlie was late again.
"What's the story?" said Ms. Noble. "Did you *forget to get out of your bed?*"
"Well, you see," said Charlie, "it's like this. . ."
"I was tidy when I started out, and I was good and early, too. But on the way. . ." (group explanation of what happens to Charlie on his way to school and what evidence he brings with him).

A Literature Lesson 7 *Charlie Best*

1
1. tidy
2. grope
3. nature
4. rumble
5. hitched

2
1. especially
2. bellowing
3. particularly
4. dreadful

3
1. prickly
2. awfully
3. wonderfully
4. truly
5. wriggly
6. horribly
7. luckily

4
1. Charlie
2. Ms. Noble
3. schoolbag
4. whistle
5. tucked
6. emptied

5
1. scooped
2. dragon
3. slippery
4. untangled
5. sewing

B Write answers to these questions on lined paper.

1. Why didn't Charlie get to school on time Monday morning?

2. What did he bring to school to prove that his story was true?

3. What proof did he have that he tripped into a river?

4. What proof did he have that he went into a forest?

5. What proof did he have that he fell into a cave?

6. On which day was Charlie on time at school?

7. Who made sure that he was on time?

C **Answer these questions about the story *Charlie Best.***

1. What is the main setting for this story?

   _____

2. Name the 2 main characters in this story.

   _____

3. Write the plot for this story. Tell about Charlie's problem and what he did. Tell about Ms. Noble. Tell about the surprise at the end of the story.

   _____

   _____

   _____

   _____

   _____

   _____

   _____

Literature Lesson 7 — Group Worksheet

Write your story so Ms. Noble says all the things she says at first. Then Charlie says all the things he says. Start the story this way:

The next Thursday Charlie was late again.
"What's the story?" said Ms. Noble.

"Did you _____

_____ ?"

"Well, you see," said Charlie, "it's like this. . ."

" _____

_____

_____

_____

_____

_____

_____

_____ . "

The Pancake Collector

Written by Jack Prelutsky

Illustrated by Rose Berlin

Theme: Collections

The Pancake Collector is a poem about an unusual collection.

Materials Needed for Lesson

1 copy of the literature anthology for each student
1 copy of blackline master 8A for each student

Materials for Optional Activity

Drawing materials

Presenting the Lesson

1. Find page 81 in your anthology. ✔

• I'll read this poem to you. Then we'll go over what it means. Listen to the whole poem.

• (Teacher reference:)

The Pancake Collector
Come visit my pancake collection,
it's unique in the civilized world.
I have pancakes of every description,
pancakes flaky and fluffy and curled.

I have pancakes of various sizes,
pancakes regular, heavy and light,
underdone pancakes and overdone pancakes,
and pancakes done perfectly right.

I have pancakes locked up in the closets,
I have pancakes on hangers and hooks.
They're in bags and in boxes and bureaus,
and pressed in the pages of books.

There are pretty ones sewn to the cushions
and tastefully pinned to the drapes.
The ceilings are coated with pancakes,
and the carpets are covered with crepes.

I have pancakes in most of my pockets,
and concealed in the linings of suits.
There are tiny ones stuffed in my mittens
and larger ones packed in my boots.

I have extras of most of my pancakes,
I maintain them in rows on these shelves,
and if you say nice things about them,
you may take a few home for yourselves.

I see that you've got to be going,
Won't you let yourselves out by the door?
It is time that I pour out the batter
and bake up a few hundred more.

2. Here's the first part of the poem:
>   Come visit my pancake collection,
>   it's unique in the civilized world.
>   I have pancakes of every description,
>   pancakes flaky and fluffy and curled.

- What kind of collection does the author have? (Call on a student. Idea: *A pancake collection.*)
- That part says that the collection is unique. **Unique** means there's nothing else like it. Tell what some of the pancakes in the collection look like. (Call on a student. Idea: *Flaky, fluffy, curled.*)

3. Here's the next part of the poem:
>   I have pancakes of various sizes,
>   pancakes regular, heavy and light,
>   underdone pancakes and overdone pancakes,
>   and pancakes done perfectly right.

- Name some of the types of pancakes the author has. (Call on individual students. Ideas: *Different sizes; underdone, overdone, perfectly done; regular, heavy, light.*)
- What would an overdone pancake be like? (Call on a student. Ideas: *Tough, dry.*)
- What would an underdone pancake be like? (Call on a student. Ideas: *Gooey, sticky.*)

4. Here's the next part:
>   I have pancakes locked up in the closets.
>   I have pancakes on hangers and hooks.
>   They're in bags and in boxes and bureaus,
>   and pressed in the pages of books.

- That part mentions a bureau. That's a dresser.
- Name some of the places the author has pancakes. (Call on individual students.
  Ideas: *In closets; on hangers and hooks; in bags, boxes, and bureaus; in books.*)

5. Here's the next part:

   > There are pretty ones sewn to the cushions
   > and tastefully pinned to the drapes.
   > The ceilings are coated with pancakes
   > and the carpets are covered with crepes.

- What a strange collection! Where are some of the pretty pancakes? (Call on individual
  students. Ideas: *On cushions, on drapes; on the ceilings; on the carpets.*)
- It says the carpets are covered with crepes. Crepes are thin, light pancakes.

6. Here's the next part:

   > I have pancakes in most of my pockets
   > and concealed in the linings of suits.
   > There are tiny ones stuffed in my mittens
   > and larger ones packed in my boots.

- Some of those pancakes are concealed in the lining of suits. That means **hidden** in the
  lining of suits.
- What are some of the other articles of clothing that conceal pancakes? (Call on a
  student. Idea: *Mittens and boots.*)

7. Here's the next part:

   > I have extras of most of my pancakes,
   > I maintain them in rows on these shelves,
   > and if you say nice things about them,
   > you may take a few home for yourselves.

- The poem says the author maintains these pancakes in rows. That means the author
  makes sure those pancakes stay in rows.

8. Here's the last part:

   > I see that you've got to be going,
   > Won't you let yourselves out by the door?
   > It is time that I pour out the batter
   > and bake up a few hundred more.

- How many more pancakes does the author plan to make? (Call on a student. Idea: *A
  few hundred.*)
- What is the batter that the author refers to? (Call on a student. Idea: *Pancake batter.*)
- I'll read the first part again. When I'm done, raise your hand if you want to read the next
  part. Listen. (Read the first stanza.)
- (Call on individual students to read the rest of the stanzas.)

Activity

1. (Distribute copies of BLM 8A to students.) Look at your worksheet.
2. (Call on a student to read the directions.)

- (Teacher reference:)

> Write a paragraph that describes the collection you would like to have most. Tell about some of the things that would be in that collection. Tell why you would really like to have the collection and what you would do with the things in the collection. You may also draw a picture of the collection you'd like to have.

- (Tell students when they should complete the assignment.)

Literature Lesson 8 *The Pancake Collector*

Write a paragraph that describes the collection you would like to have most. Tell about some of the things that would be in that collection. Tell why you would really like to have the collection and what you would do with the things in the collection. You may also draw a picture of the collection you'd like to have.

_____

_____

_____

_____

_____

_____

_____

Literature Lesson 9

Not Just Any Ring

Written by Danita Ross Haller

Illustrated by Deborah Kogan Ray

Theme: Courage

Not Just Any Ring tells of a girl's lesson in wishing for "good days."

Materials Needed for Lesson

1 copy of literature anthology for each student
1 copy of blackline master 9A for each student
Modeling clay
Sources for researching Southwest Native Americans

Materials for Optional Activities
Materials for making displays (e.g. poster board, markers, scissors, glue, etc.)

Presenting the Lesson

1. (Make copies of blackline master 9A.)

2. (Distribute copies of blackline master 9A to students.) I'll read the words in Part A. Follow along. (Read the words and explain what they mean.)

- (Teacher reference:)

1. arroyo	2. mission	3. canyon
4. earthen	5. mesa	6. boulders

- An **arroyo** is a valley that has no water in it most of the time, but when it rains, a stream flows through the arroyo.
- The **mission** in the story is a church and other buildings that were built long ago.
- A **canyon** is a narrow passage between high cliffs. Canyons are made by rivers or streams.
- Things that are **earthen** are made of clay. An earthen pot is made of clay. An earthen wall is made of clay.
- A **mesa** is a mountain with a large flat top.
- **Boulders** are very large rocks.

3. (Direct students to follow along as you read *Not Just Any Ring*. Tell students to raise their hand and ask questions about anything in the story that they don't understand.)

4. (Read to the students: *Not Just Any Ring*.)

5. (Direct students to read orally the words in columns 1 through 3 in part B.)

- (Teacher reference:)

1	2	3
1. polished	1. statue	1. arroyo
2. mesa	2. prayer	2. juniper
3. sculpture	3. blur	3. boulders
4. candles	4. plunges	4. limb
5. earthen	5. exhausted	5. towed
6. canyon		

6. (Direct the students to read the story aloud, calling on individual students to read two or three sentences at a time.)

7. (Direct students to write answers to the questions in part C of blackline master 9A.)

(Answer Key:)
1. What was Jessie's ring made of? *Silver.*
2. Where did she get the ring? Idea: *At the mission.*
3. Who took her to get the ring? Idea: *Her grandfather.*
4. What did Jessie think the ring would bring her?
   Ideas: *Good days; good luck.*
5. Why did Jessie and her grandfather take the old road home?
   Ideas: *Because it was beautiful; because it was their favorite road.*
6. What happened to the truck on the way home? *Idea: It got stuck.*
7. Jessie and her grandfather had to climb to the top of _____ .
   The mesa.
8. What did Jessie do with the ring after her grandfather slipped?
   Idea: *Threw it on the ground.*
9. What did her grandfather give to her at the end of the story? *The ring.*

Activities

1. (Divide the class into 3 groups. Each group is to make something from the story out of clay. Group 1 is to make the mission; group 2 is to make a mesa; group 3 is to make buildings for the top of the mesa.)

2. (Before groups make their models, they are to find pictures to work from and find out information about southwestern Native Americans.)

3. (Each group may also provide information about their model with a display that consists of illustrations, posters, or books.)

Literature Lesson 9 *Not Just Any Ring*

1. arroyo   2. mission   3. canyon
4. earthen   5. mesa   6. boulders

B

1
1. polished
2. mesa
3. sculpture
4. candles
5. earthen
6. canyon

2
1. statue
2. prayer
3. blur
4. plunges
5. exhausted

3
1. arroyo
2. juniper
3. boulders
4. limb
5. towed

C **Write answers to these questions on lined paper.**

1. What was Jessie's ring made of?

2. Where did she get the ring?

3. Who took her to get the ring?

4. What did Jessie think the ring would bring her?

5. Why did Jessie and her grandfather take the old road home?

6. What happened to the truck on the way home?

7. Jessie and her grandfather had to climb to the top of ███████.

8. What did Jessie do with the ring after her grandfather slipped?

9. What did her grandfather give to her at the end of the story?

Literature Lesson 10

To be presented with Lesson 100
Anthology page 128

10-1 *A Lucky Thing*

Written by Alice Schertle

Illustrated by Tony Caldwell

Theme: Perspective

A Lucky Thing is a poem about some chickens and a robin that see each other's place in the world as a lucky thing.

10-2 *The New Kid*

Written by Mike Makley

Illustrated by Kate Flanagan

Theme: Gender equality

The New Kid is a poem about a terrific new player on a kids' baseball team.

Materials Needed for Lesson 10-1

1 copy of the literature anthology for each student
1 copy of blackline master 10A for each student

Materials Needed for Lesson 10-2

1 copy of the literature anthology for each student

Presenting Lesson 10-1

1. Find page 128 in your anthology. ✔

- I'll read this poem to you. Then we'll go over what it means. Listen to the whole poem.
- (Teacher reference:)

A Lucky Thing

High
up in a hawthorn tree
a robin perched, where he could see
into a coop of wire and wood.
Inside the coop a farmer stood
flinging grain upon the ground.
Twelve fat chickens gathered round.

The robin,
singing, cocked his head
and watched the chickens being fed.

He saw it was a lucky thing
to be a chicken: Farmers bring
you golden grain, scoop after scoop,
if you're a chicken in a coop—
a lovely coop with nesting boxes
safe from cats and crows and foxes.

The chickens
in the coop could see
the bird. They heard his melody
and clucked it was a lucky thing
to be a robin who could sing
a song upon a hawthorn tree.
They watched him through the woven wire.
They saw him fly up high, and higher.

Twelve fat chickens
scratched the floor.
The farmer closed
and latched
the door.

2. Here's the first part of the poem:

> High
> up in a hawthorn tree
> a robin perched, where he could see
> into a coop of wire and wood.
> Inside the coop a farmer stood
> flinging grain upon the ground.
> Twelve fat chickens gathered round.

- Everybody, who was looking at the chickens? **(Signal.)** *A robin.*
- Where was the robin? **(Call on a student. Idea:** *In a tree.***)**
- A hawthorn tree is a small tree that has sharp thorns.
- The poem says the chickens were in a **coop.** A coop is a large cage that is made of wire and wood.
- Who can tell what flinging means? **(Call on a student. Ideas:** *Throwing, tossing.***)**
- The farmer is in the coop tossing grain for the twelve chickens.

3. Here's the next part of the poem:

> The robin,
> singing, cocked his head
> and watched the chickens being fed.
> He saw it was a lucky thing
> to be a chicken: Farmers bring
> you golden grain, scoop after scoop,
> if you're a chicken in a coop—
> a lovely coop with nesting boxes
> safe from cats and crows and foxes.

- Everybody, did the robin like the coop? (Signal.) *Yes.*
- Why did the robin think that it was a lucky thing to be a chicken? (Call on individual students. Ideas: *The farmer brought food; the coop had nice nesting boxes; the coop was a safe place.*)
- Everybody, did the robin get food served to him? (Signal.) *No.*
- Was the robin safe from cats, and crows and foxes? (Signal.) *No.*

4. Here's the next part:

> The chickens
> in the coop could see
> the bird. They heard his melody
> and clucked it was a lucky thing
> to be a robin who could sing
> a song upon a hawthorn tree.
> They watched him through the woven wire.
> They saw him fly up high, and higher.

- Why did the chickens think it was a lucky thing to be a robin? (Call on individual students. Ideas: *Because a robin could sit in a tree and sing; a robin could fly high in the sky.*)
- The chickens heard the robin's melody. That's the song the robin sang.
- What does it mean **They watched him through the woven wire?** (Call on a student. Idea: *They looked out of their cage.*)

5. Here's the last part:

> Twelve fat chickens
> scratched the floor.
> The farmer closed
> and latched
> the door.

- If the farmer latched the door, the chickens were locked in the coop. Do you think the chickens would rather be in that coop or flying the way a robin does? (Call on a student. Idea: *Flying like the robin.*)
- Who does the poem suggest is luckier, the chickens or the robin? (Call on a student. Idea: Student preference.)

6. Raise your hand if you'd like to read part of this poem.
(Call on individual students, each to read one of the stanzas.)

Activities

1. (Distribute copies of BLM 10A to students.) Follow along while I read the directions.

- You're going to write about things that might make somebody look lucky to somebody else. **Pick part A or part B for your writing.**

> Thousands of children would love to fly with Santa Claus on Christmas Eve. But Santa thinks that the children are the lucky ones on Christmas Eve.
>
> Write a paragraph. Tell why some children might think Santa is lucky. Tell why Santa might think that some children are lucky.

> Think of somebody that you think is very lucky. Write a paragraph that tells why you think that person is very lucky.
>
> Write another paragraph about somebody who might think that **you** are very lucky. Tell about some of the things you have and do that some people don't have or can't do.

2. (Tell students:) Decide if you want to do part A or part B. Then do your writing.

Presenting Lesson 10-2

1. Find page 130 in your anthology. ✔

2. I'll read this poem to you. Then we'll go over what it means. Listen to the whole poem.

- (Teacher reference:)

> ### The New Kid
>
> Our baseball team never did very much,
> we had me and PeeWee and Earl and Dutch.
> And the Oak Street Tigers always got beat
> until the new kid moved in on our street.
>
> The kid moved in with a mitt and a bat.
> and an official New York Yankee hat.
> The new kid plays shortstop or second base
> and can outrun us all in any place.
>
> The kid never muffs a grounder or fly
> no matter how hard it's hit or how high.
> And the new kid always acts quite polite,
> never yelling or spitting or starting a fight.

We were playing the league champs just last week;
they were trying to break our winning streak.
In the last inning the score was one–one,
when the new kid swung and hit a home run.

A few of the kids and their parents say
they don't believe that the new kid should play.
But she's good as me, Dutch, PeeWee, or Earl,
so we don't care that the new kid's a girl.

3. Here's the first part of the poem:

> Our baseball team never did very much,
> we had me and Pee Wee and Earl and Dutch.
> And the Oak Street Tigers always got beat
> until the new kid moved in on our street.

- The name of the team in this poem is the Oak Street Tigers.
  Everybody, what game did that team play? **(Signal.)** *Baseball.*
- How good was the team before the new kid moved in on the street? **(Call on a student.**
  Ideas: *Not very good; they always got beat.***)**

4. Here's the next part of the poem:

> The kid moved in with a mitt and a bat
> and an official New York Yankee hat.
> The new kid plays shortstop or second base
> and can outrun us all in any place.

- What 3 things did the new kid arrive with? **(Call on a student. Idea:** *A mitt, a bat, a Yankees hat.***)**
- What kind of mitt is used in baseball? **(Call on a student. Idea:** *A big, soft mitt.***)**
- Why is a baseball mitt so big and so soft? **(Call on a student. Idea:** *So it doesn't hurt when you catch the ball.***)**
- An official New York Yankee hat is just like the ones the players on the New York Yankees wear. The New York Yankees are a major-league team from New York City.
- It says the kid plays shortstop and second base. Those are two different positions that a baseball team has.
- Listen to that part again. **(Reread the second stanza.)**

5. Here's the next part:

> The kid never muffs a grounder or fly
> no matter how hard it's hit or how high.
> And the new kid always acts quite polite,
> never yelling or spitting or starting a fight.

- It says the kid never muffs a grounder or fly. A **grounder** is a ball that is hit on the ground. A fly is a ball that is hit in the air. If somebody **muffs** a ball that is coming to them, they drop it or let it go past them. The kid never muffs grounders or flies so the kid never misses any balls that come near the kid.

- Everybody, does the new kid have **good** or **bad** manners? (Signal.) *Good.*
- How do you know? (Call on a student. Ideas: *The new kid is polite; doesn't yell or fight.*)

6. Here's the next part:

> We were playing the league champs just last week;
> they were trying to break our winning streak.
> In the last inning the score was one–one,
> when the new kid swung and hit a home run.

- They were playing the league champs. That's the team that was the best team the Oak Street Tigers played last year.
- What was the score near the end of the game? (Signal.) *One–one.*
- That means each team had one run. The game was tied.
- The poem refers to a **winning streak.** That means the Tigers won a lot of games in a row, without losing any.
- The last inning is the last time the Tigers had a turn at batting. If the new kid hit a home run, the Tigers scored at least one more run.
- Listen to that part again. (**Reread the fourth stanza.**)

7. Here's the last part:

> A few of the kids and their parents say
> they don't believe that the new kid should play.
> But she's good as me, Dutch, PeeWee, or Earl,
> so we don't care that the new kid's a girl.

- What did that part tell about the new kid? (Call on a student. Ideas: *The new kid is a girl; the new kid is as good as other players; some people don't want the new kid to play on the team.*)
- Why do some people think the new kid shouldn't play? (Call on a student. Idea: *Because she's a girl.*)
- What do Dutch and Earl and PeeWee think about the new kid? (Call on a student. Ideas: *That she's a good player; they don't care that she's a girl.*)
- Why does the poem leave the part about the new kid being a girl until the very end? (Call on a student. Ideas: *So it's a surprise; it shows that things can be different from what you expect.*)

8. Raise your hand if you'd like to read part of this poem. (Call on individual students to read one of the stanzas.)

Literature Lesson 10–1 *A Lucky Thing*

You're going to write about things that might make somebody look lucky to somebody else. **Pick part A or part B for your writing.**

A Thousands of children would love to fly with Santa Claus on Christmas Eve. But Santa thinks that the children are the lucky ones on Christmas Eve.

Write a paragraph. Tell why some children might think Santa is lucky. Tell why Santa might think that some children are lucky.

_____

_____

_____

_____

_____

_____

B Think of somebody that you think is very lucky. Write a paragraph that tells why you think that person is very lucky.

Write another paragraph about somebody who might think that **you** are very lucky. Tell about some of the things you have and do that some people don't have or can't do.

_____

_____

_____

_____

_____

Literature Lesson 11

To be presented with Lesson 110
Anthology page 131

Steps

Written by Deborah M. Newton Chocolate

Illustrated by Morissa Lipstein

Theme: Overcoming differences

Steps is a story about two stepbrothers who end up being friends after having to deal with a mutual problem.

Materials Needed for Lesson

1 copy of the literature anthology for each student
1 copy of blackline masters 11A and 11B for each student
1 copy of blackline masters 11C and 11D for each 12 students
Scissors
Lined paper
Optional: Heavy paper for copying 11C and 11D

Presenting the Lesson

1. (Make copies of blackline masters.)
2. (Distribute copies of blackline masters 11A and 11B to students. Direct students to read orally the words in column 1 of part A. Explain what the words mean.)
- (Teacher reference:)

1
1. hardware store
2. stepbrother
3. obedient
4. scanned
5. pleaded
6. vacant

- A **hardware store** is a place where you can buy tools and materials for building or repairing things. You can find things to repair a lawn mower at a hardware store.
- If one of your parents marries someone who already has a son, that boy is your **stepbrother.**
- If you are **obedient,** you follow the rules you're supposed to follow. You go to school on time, you do what your parents say, and you follow all your family rules.
- When you **scan** something, you look it over very quickly.

- **Pleaded** is another word for **begged.** If you beg for help, you plead for help.
- **Vacant** is another word for **empty.** A vacant house is an empty house.
3. (Direct students to read orally the words in columns 2 through 4.)
- (Teacher reference:)

2
1. pedaled
2. Rudy
3. loose
4. Sonny
5. cousin
6. unpacking

3
1. Jamal
2. dared
3. pitching
4. towards
5. knelt

4
1. Emergency Squad
2. disappointment
3. prepared
4. neon
5. hospital
6. screw

4. (Direct students to read the story aloud, calling on individual students to read two or three sentences at a time. Tell students to raise their hand and ask a question about anything in the story that they don't understand.)
5. (After students have completed the story, direct them to write answers to the questions in part B of blackline master 11A.)

(Answer Key:)
1. At the beginning of the story, who got into an argument over the sewing machine?
   Jamal and Sonny.
2. Who settled the argument?
   Their dad.
3. What did Jamal want to do in the vacant lot?
   Idea: *Ride his bike on the hills.*
4. What had once happened to Sonny when he was riding on dirt hills?
   Idea: *He'd broken his arm.*
5. What happened to Jamal in the vacant lot?
   Ideas: *Flew off his bike; broke his leg.*
6. Where did Sonny go for help?
   Grocery store.
7. What did Sonny say he'd do to keep Jamal in shape?
   Idea: *Practice his pitching arm.*

Retelling the Story

1. I'm going to call on individual students to retell different parts of this story. Who wants to start with the title and tell the first part of the story? (Call on a student. After the student has told the first part of the story, call on another student to start there and tell more of the story. Continue until the story has been retold. Praise accounts that present the important details of the story.)
2. (Repeat the procedure, calling on individual students.)

Optional—New Ending

- Raise your hand if you can tell the story with a different ending. (Call on a student.) Start where the boys are riding their bikes on the hills at the vacant lot and tell the new ending.

Optional—Dramatization

- What part of the story do you like the best? (Call on individual students.)
- (Select one of the scenes.) Let's act out that part. (Assign students to play the roles of the characters and act out the selected scene.)

Literary Elements

1. Find part C on your worksheet. ✔
- You're going to answer questions about the setting, the characters, and the plot for the story *Steps.*
2. Item 1 asks: What is the main setting for this story? Everybody, write the answer to item 1. Raise your hand when you've done that much. (Observe students and give feedback.)
- What's the answer to item 1? (Call on a student. Idea: *Sonny and Jamal's house; neighborhood.*)
3. Item 2 says: Name the two main characters in this story. Everybody, write the answer to item 2. Raise your hand when you've done that much.
   (Observe students and give feedback.)
- What's the answer to item 2? (Call on a student.) *Sonny and Jamal.*
4. Item 3 says: Write the plot for this story. Tell who Sonny and Jamal are. Tell about their problem. Tell what happened to Jamal, and what Sonny did. Tell how Jamal's feelings changed. Write the plot. Raise your hand when you're done.
   (Observe students and give feedback.)
- (Call on individual students to read the plot. Praise accounts that provide the information that the item specifies.)

Activities

Role playing

1. (Reproduce blackline masters 11C and 11D. Then cut the copies into "cards," keeping the cards in two separate piles.)

- (Each group of about 4 students draws one card from the situation pile [11D] and two cards from the people pile [11C]. Students are to discuss the characters and the circumstances of the plot. After they get your okay, they are to specify the details of their play. Then they are to make up a play that has the characters and possibly a narrator. The characters may include others in the family. The play is to show how the characters act when they have their problem and then how the problem is solved.)

How big is the problem?

2. (Discuss the pattern of problems that families and friends have. Point out that little differences disappear when people share a big problem.)

- (Pose this situation in which there is a disagreement: Beth and James quarrel about which TV program to watch. A big problem could make them thankful to watch **any** TV program. Ask students to suggest a problem that would require both James and Beth to get involved in issues far more important than which program to watch.)

- (Make a list of the events that students suggest. Optionally assign a group to put on a play or write a story that is based on one of these events.)

Literature Lesson 11 *Steps*

1
1. hardware store
2. stepbrother
3. obedient
4. scanned
5. pleaded
6. vacant

2
1. pedaled
2. Rudy
3. loose
4. Sonny
5. cousin
6. unpacking

3
1. Jamal
2. dared
3. pitching
4. towards
5. knelt

4
1. Emergency Squad
2. disappointment
3. prepared
4. neon
5. hospital
6. screw

B Write answers to these questions on lined paper.

1. At the beginning of the story, who got into an argument over the sewing machine?

2. Who settled the argument?

3. What did Jamal want to do in the vacant lot?

4. What had once happened to Sonny when he was riding on dirt hills?

5. What happened to Jamal in the vacant lot?

6. Where did Sonny go for help?

7. What did Sonny say he'd do to keep Jamal in shape?

C **Answer these questions about the story _Steps_.**

1. What is the main setting for this story? _____

_____

2. Name the 2 main characters in this story. _____

_____

3. Write the plot for this story. Tell who Sonny and Jamal are. Tell about their problem. Tell what happened to Jamal, and what Sonny did. Tell how Jamal's feelings changed. _____

_____

_____

_____

_____

_____

_____

_____

father

mother

brother

sister

friend

friend

They do not agree
about what to eat.

One of them bosses
the other around.

One of them thinks that the
other one gets special
treatment.

They don't like to share
something they're supposed
to share.

Literature Lesson 12

Lesson 12-1 to be presented with Lesson 120
Anthology page 144

Lesson 12-2 can be presented at a later time.

12-1 *The Soup Stone*

Retold by Maria Leach

Illustrated by Karen Bauman

Themes: Combined efforts; we often have more than we realize.

The Soup Stone demonstrates that with a little help from everyone, great things can be accomplished.

12-2 *Julie Rescues Big Mack*

Written by Roger Hall

Illustrated by Joy Antonie

Themes: Clues; mistreating animals

Julie Rescues Big Mack is a story about a young girl who saves the life of a friend's kidnapped dog.

Materials Needed for Lesson 12-1

1 copy of the literature anthology for each student
1 copy of blackline masters 12A and 12B for each student
Lined paper

Materials Needed for Lesson 12-2

1 copy of blackline master 12C for each student

Presenting Lesson 12-1

1. (Make copies of blackline masters.)
2. (Distribute copies of blackline masters 12A and 12B to students. Direct students to read orally the words in column 1 of part A. Explain what the words mean.)
- (Teacher reference:)

1
1. spare
2. eye
3. ladle
4. formula
5. tale

- If you can **spare** something, it is something you don't need. If you can spare some salt, you have some salt that you don't need.
- When you **eye** something, you look at it closely.
- A **ladle** is a huge curved spoon that is used for serving soup.
- A **formula** is a rule for doing something. It may be a rule for cooking something.
- A **tale** is a story that is probably not true.

3. (Direct students to read orally the words in columns 2 and 3.)

- (Teacher reference:)

2	3
1. kindness	1. flavor
2. politely	2. longingly
3. carrots	3. potatoes
4. stirring	4. finishing
5. fistful	5. thicken
6. onion	

4. (Direct students to read *The Soup Stone,* calling on individual students to read two or three sentences at a time. Tell students to raise their hand and ask a question about anything in the story that they don't understand.)

5. (After students have completed the story, direct them to write answers to the questions in part B of blackline master 12A.)

(Answer Key:)

1. Who had the idea for making soup?
   The soldier.
2. What was the first thing that went into the water?
   The stone.
3. Name 4 other things they added to the water.
   Ideas (any 4): *Salt, carrots, potatoes, onions, cabbage, rabbits.*
4. Who had the onion?
   (The next-door) neighbor.
5. Who had the rabbits?
   The oldest son.
6. What did the soldier give the woman at the end of the story?
   The stone.
7. Where did the soldier get another one?
   Ideas: *On the road; outside the next village.*

Retelling the Story

1. I'm going to call on individual students to retell different parts of this story. Who wants to start with the title and tell the first part of the story? (Call on a student. After the student has told the first part of the story, call on another student to start there and tell more of the story. Continue until the story has been retold. Praise accounts that present the important details of the story.)
2. (Repeat the procedure, calling on individual students.)

Optional—Dramatization

- What part of the story do you like the best? (Call on individual students.)
- (Select one of the scenes.) Let's act out that part. (Assign students to play the roles of the characters and act out the selected scene.)

Literary Elements

1. Find part C on your worksheet. ✔
- You're going to answer questions about the setting, the characters, and the plot for the story *The Soup Stone.*
2. Item 1 asks: What is the main setting for this story? Everybody, write the answer to item 1. Raise your hand when you've done that much. (Observe students and give feedback.)
- What's the answer to item 1? (Call on a student. Idea: *Farmer's house.*)
3. Item 2 says: Name the two main characters in this story. The main characters are one person and one object. Everybody, write the answer to item 2. Raise your hand when you've done that much. (Observe students and give feedback.)
- What's the answer to item 2? (Call on a student. Idea: *A soldier and a soup stone.*)
4. Item 3 says: Write the plot for this story on your lined paper. Tell about the soldier's problem. Tell how he meets the farmer. Tell what they did with the soup stone. Tell how the soup was made. Write the plot. Raise your hand when you're done. (Observe students and give feedback.)
- (Call on individual students to read the plot. Praise accounts that provide the information that the item specifies.)

Fables

1. Find part D on your worksheet. ✔

• You learned that a fable is one type of literature. A fable is a special kind of fiction. It gives the reader a lesson or a message.

2. You just read the fable about the soup stone. The lesson is **Big changes can happen in little steps.**

• Everybody, say that lesson. Get ready. (Signal.) *Big changes can happen in little steps.*

• In the story, how did the soldier start the soup? (Call on a student. Idea: *With water and a stone.*)

• How did the water turn into soup? (Call on a student. Idea: *Adding one thing at a time.*)

• What was the soup like when it was done? (Call on a student. Idea: *Good, tasty.*)

3. (Tell the students when they should do the items in part D.)

4. (After the students complete the items, do a workcheck. For each item: Read the item. Call on a student to say the answer. If the answer is wrong, say the correct answer.)

Answer Key: **1.** Idea: Big changes can happen in small steps. **2.** Idea: With water and a stone **3.** Idea: By adding things **4.** Idea: Tasty

Comparison: Time Period

1. Find part E on your worksheet. ✔

• You read a very old story called *The Soup Stone.* You can tell the story is old from some of the things in it. For example, the soldier is walking home from the war. In a story that takes place today, the soldier might go home in a plane or on a ship.

2. You're going to write a list of ways the story could be different if it took place today. Four things about the story are shown in part E. For each item, write something different that could be in a story that takes place today.

3. The first item is: The soldier walked up to a house to ask for food. Write how that part of the story could be different in a story that takes place today. (Observe students and give feedback.)

• (After students have finished item 1, call on individual students to read what they wrote. Praise good responses.)

4. The next item is: The people cooked over a fire. Write how that could be different in a story that takes place today. (Observe students and give feedback.)

• (After students have finished item 2, call on individual students to read what they wrote. Praise good responses.)

5. The next item is: The farmer's son hunted for meat. Write how that might be different in a story that takes place today. (Observe students and give feedback.)

• (After students have finished item 3, call on individual students to read what they wrote. Praise good responses.)

6. The last item is: The people kept carrots under a bench. Tell how that might be different in a story that takes place today. (Observe students and give feedback.)

• (After students have finished item 4, call on individual students to read what they wrote. Praise good responses.)

Activities

Recipes

1. (Discuss the ingredients of the stone soup. Have the students identify the ingredient that did not make the soup better and did not make it worse.) [Answer: *The stone.*]

- (Direct each group to make up a recipe that works the same way. Groups could make recipes for: a clothespin salad, a magnet stew, or a seashell soup. Each group could read its recipe to the class.)

Group effort

2. (Discuss the process of making the soup. Ask:) Did any person have all the ingredients that were needed to make the soup? (Point out that when they shared what they had, they made a fine soup.)

3. (Assign groups of about 4 to write an ending to this story:) Four neighbors complained because there was no bridge across the stream. Ms. Baker had some boards. Mr. Green had lots of nails.

- (Students are to name some of the other things they would need to make the bridge. Then each group is to make up a story that tells how the neighbors worked together to build the bridge.)

Presenting Read-to Lesson 12-2

1. (Make copies of blackline master 12C.)
2. (Direct students to listen as you read *Julie Rescues Big Mack.* Tell students to raise their hand and ask a question about anything in the story that they don't understand.)
3. (Read to the students: *Julie Rescues Big Mack.* See pages 157–162 of this guide.)
4. (Distribute copies of blackline master 12C to students. Direct students to write answers to the questions on blackline master 12C.)

(Answer Key:)
1. Who owned Big Mack? *Mr. Mason.*
2. Why couldn't Julie have her own dog? Ideas: *Her brother is allergic to dogs; her dad thinks they are a nuisance to take care of; they take up room in the car.*
3. What did the books that Julie got from the library tell about? *Dogs.*
4. Where did Julie sometimes go to help with animals? *Animal Shelter.*
5. Why was Mr. Mason upset one day? Idea: *Big Mack had been stolen.*
6. What did Julie hear that led her to the old barn? Idea: *Sad howling.*
7. Where did she go to get help? *Animal Shelter.*
8. What did they find inside the barn? *Big Mack (in a wire cage).*
9. What made them think he had been in a fight?
   Idea: *He had cuts on his legs and across his back.*
10. Where did they take Big Mack? *Animal Shelter.*
11. Which person did Julie call? *Mr. Mason.*
12. At the end of the story, what did Mr. Mason tell Julie she could do? Ideas: *Come and visit Mack; take him for walks; groom him; bathe him; be an "aunt" to him.*

Activities

1. (Explain:) Mr. Mason said that "When a dog behaves badly, it's usually the fault of the owner." Sometimes, a dog behaves badly because of things that don't have to do with the owner. After Big Mack had his bad experience, he might behave badly in some situations. Those situations may make him very angry or very afraid. Describe those situations and tell what Big Mack is thinking and why he is behaving badly. Also tell what Mr. Mason or Julie could do to make these situations easier for Big Mack.

Clues

2. (Explain:) The story doesn't really tell what happened to Big Mack. It uses clues. Here are some things that probably could not have happened. Tell about the clues that let you know why each one is impossible.

- Big Mack was not stolen. He just decided to go live in the barn.
- Big Mack was not in a fight. He just got some scratches from jumping over a fence.
- Big Mack was not being starved. He just decided not to eat for a while.

Literature Lesson 12-1 *The Soup Stone*

A

1
1. spare
2. eye
3. ladle
4. formula
5. tale

2
1. kindness
2. politely
3. carrots
4. stirring
5. fistful
6. onion

3
1. flavor
2. longingly
3. potatoes
4. finishing
5. thicken

B **Write answers to these questions on lined paper.**

1. Who had the idea for making soup?

2. What was the first thing that went into the water?

3. Name 4 other things they added to the water.

4. Who had the onion?

5. Who had the rabbits?

6. What did the soldier give the woman at the end of the story?

7. Where did the soldier get another one?

C **Answer these questions about the story *The Soup Stone*.**

1. What is the main setting for this story? _____

2. Name the two main characters in this story. _____

_____

3. Write the two plots for this story on your lined paper. Tell about the soldier's problem. Tell how he meets the farmer. Tell what they did with the soup stone. Tell how the soup was made.

D **Answer these questions.**

1. What is the lesson of the fable about the soup stone?

_____

_____

2. In the story *The Soup Stone,* how did the soldier start the soup?

_____

3. How did the water turn into soup?

_____

4. What was the soup like when it was done? _____

E **Write ways that the story *The Soup Stone* could be different if it took place today.**

1. The soldier walked up to a house to ask for food. _____

_____

2. The people cooked over a fire. _____

_____

3. The farmer's son hunted for meat. _____

_____

4. The people kept carrots under a bench. _____

_____

Literature Lesson 12-2 *Julie Rescues Big Mack*

1. Who owned Big Mack?

   _____

2. Why couldn't Julie have her own dog?

   _____

3. What did the books that Julie got from the library tell about?

   _____

4. Where did Julie sometimes go to help with animals?

   _____

5. Why was Mr. Mason upset one day?

   _____

6. What did Julie hear that led her to the old barn?

   _____

7. Where did she go to get help?

   _____

8. What did they find inside the barn?

   _____

9. What made them think he had been in a fight?

   _____

10. Where did they take Big Mack?

    _____

11. Which person did Julie call?

    _____

12. At the end of the story, what did Mr. Mason tell Julie she could do?

    _____

Literature Lesson 13

To be presented with Lesson 130
Anthology page 150

Amelia Bedelia

Written by Peggy Parish

Illustrated by Fritz Siebel

Theme: Unclear instructions

Amelia Bedelia is a funny story about how directions can be misinterpreted.

Materials Needed for Lesson

> 1 copy of the literature anthology for each student
> 1 copy of blackline masters 13A and 13B for each student
> 1 copy of blackline master 13C for each 4 students
> Lined paper
> Drawing materials

Presenting the Lesson

1. (Make copies of blackline masters.)
2. (Distribute copies of blackline masters 13A and 13B to students. Direct students to read orally the words in column 1 of Part A. Explain what the words mean.)
- (Teacher reference:)

1
1. deliver
2. market
3. unusual
4. air
5. trim
6. lemon meringue

- **Deliver** means **bring.** Somebody who delivers the mail brings the mail.
- A **market** is a store that sells groceries.
- **Unusual** means **strange** or **not ordinary.** An unusual event is a strange event.
- When you **air** something, you put it where fresh air can reach it.
- When you **trim** something, you get rid of parts that are not needed. You can trim a steak by cutting the fat from it.
- **Lemon meringue** is a very tasty kind of pie.

3. (Direct students to read orally the words in columns 2 through 4.)

- (Teacher reference:)

2	3	4
1. Amelia Bedelia	1. happily	1. steak
2. poured	2. lace	2. container
3. scissors	3. Rogers	3. snipped
4. furniture	4. switched	4. hurried
5. undust	5. cared	5. ribbon
6. unlight	6. powder	6. drapes
7. unscrewed	7. rice	7. dusted

4. (Direct students to read the story aloud, calling on individual students to read two or three sentences at a time. Tell students to raise their hand and ask a question about anything in the story that they don't understand.)

5. (After students have completed the story, direct them to write answers to the questions in part B of blackline master 13A.)

> (Answer Key:)
>
> 1. What did Mrs. Rogers want Amelia to do when she told her to change the towels in the green bathroom?
>   Idea: *Replace the towels with fresh towels.*
> 2. How did Amelia change the towels?
>   Ideas: *She cut them; she snipped them; she reshaped them.*
> 3. How did Amelia dust the furniture?
>   Idea: *She covered the furniture with dusting powder.*
> 4. What did Mrs. Rogers want Amelia to do when she said to draw the drapes when the sun came in? *Idea: To shut the drapes.*
> 5. How did Amelia put the lights out?
>   Idea: *She unscrewed the lightbulbs and hung them out to air.*
> 6. How did she measure two cups of rice?
>   Idea: *She stacked 2 cups full of rice and measured how tall they were.*
> 7. How did she dress the chicken?
>   Idea: *She put clothes on it.*
> 8. Who wanted to fire Amelia? *Mrs. Rogers.*
> 9. Who wanted to keep her? *Mr. Rogers.*
> 10. Why? Idea: *He liked her lemon-meringue pie.*

Retelling the Story

1. I'm going to call on individual students to retell different parts of this story. Who wants to start with the title and tell the first part of the story? (Call on a student. After the student has told the first part of the story, call on another student to start there and tell more of the story. Continue until the story has been retold. Praise accounts that present the important details of the story.)

2. (Repeat the procedure, calling on individual students.)

Optional—New Ending

- Raise your hand if you can tell the story with a different ending. (Call on a student.) Start where Mr. and Mrs. Rogers return home and tell the new ending.

Optional—Dramatization

- What part of the story do you like the best? (Call on individual students.)
- (Select one of the scenes.) Let's act out that part. (Assign students to play the roles of the characters and act out the selected scene.)

Literary Elements

1. Find part C on your worksheet. ✔
- You're going to answer questions about the setting, the characters, and the plot for the story *Amelia Bedelia.*
2. Item 1 asks: What is the main setting for this story? Everybody, write the answer to item 1. Raise your hand when you've done that much.
   (Observe students and give feedback.)
- What's the answer to item 1? (Call on a student. Idea: *The Rogers' house.*)
3. Item 2 says: Name the main character in this story. Everybody, write the answer to item 2. Raise your hand when you've done that much.
   (Observe students and give feedback.)
- Everybody, what's the answer to item 2? (Signal.) *Amelia Bedelia.*
4. Item 3 says: Write the plot for this story on lined paper. Tell about Amelia Bedelia's new job. Tell how she did her job. Tell why Mr. and Mrs. Rogers didn't fire Amelia Bedelia. Write the plot. Raise your hand when you're done.
   (Observe students and give feedback.)
- (Call on individual students to read the plot. Praise accounts that provide the information that the item specifies.)

Story Themes

1. It is possible to write many different stories that have the same theme. Here's a theme: Big changes can happen in small steps.
- Here's another theme: Helping others leads to friendship.
- Here's another theme: You can't fool everybody all the time.
2. Find part D on your worksheet. ✔

- (Teacher reference:)

> - Big changes can happen in small steps.
> - Helping others leads to friendship.
> - You can't fool everybody all the time.

For each title below, write the theme that fits the story.
1. *Why Leopard Has Black Spots*
2. *Steps*
3. *The Soup Stone*
4. *The Emperor's New Clothes*
5. Pick one of the themes in the box above. On lined paper, write the plot for a story that has that theme.

- The themes I just talked about are in the box. Follow along while I read the instructions below the box: For each title below, write the theme that fits the story.
- Do items 1 through 4. Raise your hand when you've done that much. (Observe students and give feedback.)
- Check your work.
- (Call on a student to read and answer item 1.)
- (Repeat for items 2–4.)

Answer Key: **1.** You can't fool everybody all the time.   **2.** Helping others leads to friendship.   **3.** Big changes can happen in small steps.   **4.** You can't fool everybody all the time.

3. Follow along while I read item 5: Pick one of the themes in the box above. On lined paper, write the plot for a story that has that theme.
- (Tell students when they should complete the assignment.)
- (After students have finished, call on individual students to read what they wrote. Praise plots that are consistent with the selected theme.)

Activities

More than one meaning

1. (Students are to work in groups of about 4. Pass out copies of blackline master 13C to each group. Each group picks one or two items from the blackline master, discusses what their pictures will show, and makes illustrations. Each group could also write a little story that tells about the confusion.)

Literature Lesson 13 *Amelia Bedelia*

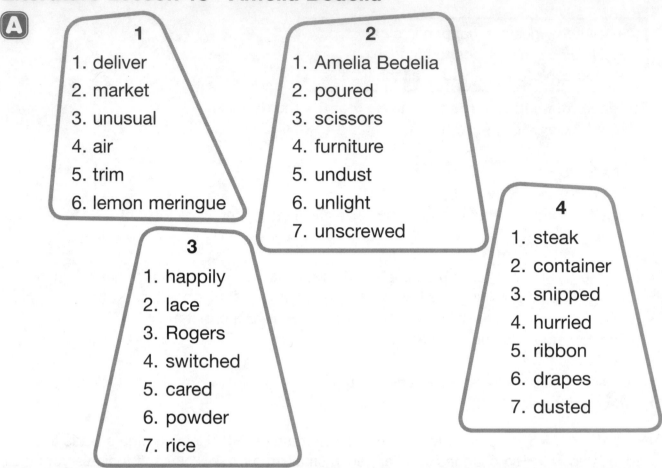

A

1
1. deliver
2. market
3. unusual
4. air
5. trim
6. lemon meringue

2
1. Amelia Bedelia
2. poured
3. scissors
4. furniture
5. undust
6. unlight
7. unscrewed

3
1. happily
2. lace
3. Rogers
4. switched
5. cared
6. powder
7. rice

4
1. steak
2. container
3. snipped
4. hurried
5. ribbon
6. drapes
7. dusted

B **Write answers to these questions on lined paper.**

1. What did Mrs. Rogers want Amelia to do when she told her to change the towels in the green bathroom?

2. How did Amelia change the towels?

3. How did Amelia dust the furniture?

4. What did Mrs. Rogers want Amelia to do when she said to draw the drapes when the sun came in?

5. How did Amelia put the lights out?

6. How did she measure two cups of rice?

7. How did she dress the chicken?

8. Who wanted to fire Amelia?

9. Who wanted to keep her?

10. Why?

C **Answer these questions about the story *Amelia Bedelia.***

1. What is the main setting for this story? _____

   _____

2. Name the main character in this story. _____

3. Write the plot for this story on lined paper. Tell about Amelia Bedelia's new job. Tell how she did her job. Tell why Mr. and Mrs. Rogers didn't fire Amelia Bedelia.

D **Here are three story themes:**

- Big changes can happen in small steps.
- Helping others leads to friendship.
- You can't fool everybody all the time.

For each title below, write the theme that fits the story.

1. Why Leopard Has Black Spots

   _____

2. Steps

   _____

3. The Soup Stone

   _____

4. The Emperor's New Clothes

   _____

5. Pick one of the themes in the box above. On lined paper, write the plot for a story that has that theme.

Literature Lesson 13 — Group Worksheet

1. She said that she was going to beat the eggs.
   Draw three different pictures showing her beating the eggs.
   One of them can be the right way.

2. It didn't take them long to trim the Christmas tree.
   Draw two pictures.

3. She told the others that she would change the baby.
   Draw two pictures.

4. At the end of the week she was broke and had no change.
   Draw two pictures.

5. Her mother told her to stamp the envelope.
   Draw two pictures.

My (Wow!) Summer Vacation

Written by Susan Cornell Poskanzer

Illustrated by Meryl Henderson

Theme: Achieving personal goals

My (Wow!) Summer Vacation shows how things you think you won't like can actually end up being the most fun.

Materials Needed for Lesson

1 copy of the literature anthology for each student
1 copy of blackline masters 14A and 14B for each student
Lined paper
Drawing material
Reference material (books, maps, CD-ROMs) on the Colorado River

Presenting the Lesson

1. (Make copies of blackline masters 14A and 14B.)
2. (Distribute copies of blackline masters 14A and 14B to students. Direct students to read orally the words in columns 1 and 2 of part A. Explain what the words mean.)
- (Teacher reference:)

1	2
1. Colorado River	1. fossils
2. Grand Canyon	2. moped
3. contraption	3. sardines
4. gila monster	4. trickle
5. brittlebush	5. jinx
6. New Jersey	6. pontoons
7. shimmering	7. Arizona
8. scorpions	8. launch

- The **Colorado River** is a river that goes from the state of Colorado all the way through California to the Pacific Ocean.
- The **Grand Canyon** is a spectacular place where the Colorado River is a mile below the top part of the canyon.
- **Contraption** is another word for **device.**
- A **gila monster** is a colorful poisonous lizard that lives in the desert.

- **Brittlebush** is a desert plant that has yellow flowers.
- **New Jersey** is a state on the east coast of the United States.
- **Shimmering** is another word for **glistening** or **glimmering.**
- **Scorpions** are members of the spider family. Scorpions are poisonous.
- **Fossils** are remains of animals that have turned to stone.
- When you **mope,** you don't have much energy and you don't feel happy.
- **Sardines** are small fish.
- A **trickle** of water is a very slow stream of water.
- Something that is a **jinx** brings bad luck.
- **Pontoons** are large hollow tubes that float in water. Some boats float on pontoons.
- **Arizona** is a state in the western part of the United States.
- When you **launch** a boat, you set it in the water.

3. (Direct students to read orally the words in columns 3 through 5.)
- (Teacher reference:)

3
1. Havasu
2. Honeybunch
3. Nankoweap
4. Owen

4
1. miracles
2. guidebook
3. hiccupped
4. lurched
5. muscular
6. shooed
7. gross
8. ledges

5
1. Badger Creek Rapid
2. Diamond Creek
3. Vulcan's Anvil
4. Lee's Ferry

4. (Direct students to read the story aloud, calling on individual students to read two or three sentences at a time. Tell students to raise their hand and ask a question about anything in the story that they don't understand.)

5. (After students have completed the story, direct them to write answers to the questions in part B of blackline master 14A.)

(Answer Key:)

1. **What was the narrator's trip name in this story?**
   Foo Foo.

2. **Where did she live?**
   New Jersey.

3. **Where did she and her parents go on vacation?**
   Ideas: *To the Grand Canyon; Arizona; Colorado River.*

4. **Who were the guides?**
   Owen and P.J.

5. **What were Foo Foo's goals for the trip?**
   3 ideas: *1. See some neat fossils; 2. Hang on to lucky baseball hat; 3. Come home alive.*

6. **What did the rafters do with their garbage?**
   Idea: *Dragged it behind their raft.*

7. **Name 3 animals that Foo Foo saw on the trip.**
   Any 3: *Sheep, mule deer, bats, rattlesnake, hummingbird.*

8. **Name 3 other interesting things Foo Foo saw on the trip.**
   Ideas (any 3 not mentioned in item 7): *2 huge sheep; rapids; a mule deer; bats; blood-red rocks; a cavern with fossils; a rattlesnake; a hummingbird; etc.*

9. **What did Foo Foo lose?**
   Her lucky baseball cap.

10. **What did the rafters see in the cavern?**
    Fossils.

11. **What did Foo Foo do for good luck before going through Lava Falls?**
    Idea: *Kissed an ugly black rock (Vulcan's Anvil).*

12. **What did the rafters find in the water?**
    Ideas: *Her baseball cap; garbage; juice cans; water bottle; pants.*

13. **What goal did Foo Foo add to her list at the end of the story?**
    Idea: *Come back and visit the Grand Canyon.*

Retelling the Story

1. I'm going to call on individual students to retell different parts of this story. Who wants to start with the title and tell the first part of the story? (Call on a student. After the student has told the first part of the story, call on another student to start there and tell more of the story. Continue until the story has been retold. Praise accounts that present the important details of the story.)

2. (Repeat the procedure, calling on individual students.)

Optional—New Ending

- Raise your hand if you can tell the story with a different ending. (Call on a student.) Start where the raft enters Lava Falls Rapid and tell the new ending.

Optional—Dramatization

- What part of the story do you like the best? (Call on individual students.)
- (Select one of the scenes.) Let's act out that part. (Assign students to play the roles of the characters and act out the selected scene.)

Literary Elements

1. Find part C on your worksheet. ✔
- You're going to answer questions about the setting, the characters, and the plot for the story *My (Wow!) Summer Vacation.*
2. Item 1 asks: What is the main setting for this story? Everybody, write the answer to item 1. Raise your hand when you've done that much.
   (Observe students and give feedback.)
- What's the answer to item 1? (Call on a student. Idea: *The Grand Canyon.*)
3. Item 2 says: Name the main character in this story. Everybody, write the answer to item 2. Raise your hand when you've done that much.
   (Observe students and give feedback.)
- What's the answer to item 2? (Call on a student. Idea: *A girl named Foo Foo.*)
4. Item 3 says: Write the plot for this story on lined paper. Tell about the family's vacation plans. Tell why Foo Foo didn't want to go. Tell about the vacation. Tell how Foo Foo's feelings changed. Write the plot. Raise your hand when you're done. (Observe students and give feedback.)
- (Call on individual students to read the plot. Praise accounts that provide the information that the item specifies.)

Story Themes

1. You learned that it's possible to write many different stories that have the same theme. Here's a theme: People often fear the unknown.
- Here's another theme: Don't judge people too quickly.
- Here's another theme: People aren't always who they pretend to be.
2. Find part D on your worksheet. ✔
- (Teacher reference:)

> - People often fear the unknown.
> - Don't judge people too quickly.
> - People aren't always who they pretend to be.

For each title below, write the theme that fits the story.
1. *Steps*
2. *My (Wow!) Summer Vacation*
3. *Charlie Best*
4. *Boar Out There*
5. *The Emperor's New Clothes*
6. Pick one of the themes in the box above. On lined paper, write the plot for a story that has that theme.

- The themes I just talked about are in the box. Follow along while I read the instructions below the box: For each title below, write the theme that fits the story.
- Do items 1 through 5. Raise your hand when you've done that much. (Observe students and give feedback.)
- Check your work.
- (Call on a student to read and answer item 1.)
- (Repeat for items 2–5.)

Answer Key: **1.** Don't judge people too quickly.   **2.** People often fear the unknown.
3. Don't judge people too quickly.   **4.** People often fear the unknown.   **5.** People aren't always who they pretend to be.

3. Follow along while I read item 6: Pick one of the themes in the box above. On lined paper, write the plot for a story that has that theme.
- (Tell students when they should complete the assignment.)
- (After students have finished, call on individual students to read what they wrote. Praise plots that are consistent with the selected theme.)

Activities

Favorite vacations

1. (Direct students to write about their favorite vacation:) You can either tell about a vacation you had or one that you dream about having. Write about something that is possible.

Group map

2. (Direct groups of about 4 students to make a map of the story:) Look up the Colorado River in reference books. Find a good map. Foo Foo saw some unusual things and unusual animals. Show these animals and things on your map. Paste pictures and descriptions on the map. Use arrows to show where you would see them.
- (Groups may make a presentation to the class and describe the trip down the Colorado River, pointing out the important things they would see.)

Literature Lesson 14 *My (Wow!) Summer Vacation*

A

1
1. Colorado River
2. Grand Canyon
3. contraption
4. gila monster
5. brittlebush
6. New Jersey
7. shimmering
8. scorpions

2
1. fossils
2. moped
3. sardines
4. trickle
5. jinx
6. pontoons
7. Arizona
8. launch

4
1. miracles
2. guidebook
3. hiccuped
4. lurched
5. muscular
6. shooed
7. gross
8. ledges

3
1. Havasu
2. Honeybunch
3. Nankoweap
4. Owen

5
1. Badger Creek Rapid
2. Diamond Creek
3. Vulcan's Anvil
4. Lee's Ferry

B **Write answers to these questions on lined paper.**

1. What was the narrator's trip name in this story?

2. Where did she live?

3. Where did she and her parents go on vacation?

4. Who were the guides?

5. What were Foo Foo's goals for the trip?

6. What did the rafters do with their garbage?

7. Name 3 animals that Foo Foo saw on the trip.

8. Name 3 other interesting things Foo Foo saw on the trip.

9. What did Foo Foo lose?

10. What did the rafters see in the cavern?

11. What did she do for good luck before going through Lava Falls?

12. What did the rafters find in the water?

13. What goal did Foo Foo add to her list at the end of the story?

C **Answer these questions about the story**
My (Wow!) Summer Vacation.

1. What is the main setting for this story? _____

_____

2. Name the main character in this story. _____

3. Write the plot for this story on lined paper. Tell about the family's vacation plans. Tell why Foo Foo didn't want to go. Tell about the vacation. Tell how Foo Foo's feelings changed.

D **Here are three story themes:**

- People often fear the unknown.
- Don't judge people too quickly.
- People aren't always who they pretend to be.

For each title below, write the theme that fits the story.

1. Steps

_____

2. My (Wow!) Summer Vacation

_____

3. Charlie Best

_____

4. Boar Out There

_____

5. The Emperor's New Clothes

_____

6. Pick one of the themes in the box above. On lined paper, write the plot for a story that has that theme.

Literature Lesson 15

To be presented with Lesson 140
Anthology page 209

The Story of Daedalus and Icarus

Written by Fran Lehr

Illustrated by Antonio Castro

Theme: Disobedience

The Story of Daedalus and Icarus is a play based on a Greek myth that demonstrates consequences of disobedience.

Materials Needed for Lesson

1 copy of the literature anthology for each student
1 copy of blackline master 15A for the teacher and for each student
1 copy of blackline master 15B for each student
Modest costumes, stage settings, and props

Presenting the Lesson

1. This is a play that we're going to read several times and then put on. When we put on the play, students will act the parts of the characters in the play. Those students will read the lines for the characters they play.

2. A play is written a different way from a story. The play has headings. The headings tell who is talking or doing something. The passage that follows the heading tells what the person says or does.

- The first part of the play tells who the characters are, when and where the play takes place and what is happening when the first scene opens. Follow along while I read the list of characters in this play: three chorus members, Daedalus, Icarus, King Minos, two guards and the Minotaur (pronunciation key: DAY-du-lus; ICK-u-rus; MY-nu-tor).

- The three chorus members are not actors in the play. They talk to the audience and tell about things the audience needs to know. The chorus members are like three narrators.

3. This play has three acts. Each act takes place in a different setting. Listen to the description for Act 1.

Time:

Over two thousand years ago.

Setting:

A seashore on the island of Crete. In the background is a rock cliff. In the middle of the cliff is the entrance to a large maze. On each side of the entrance stands a GUARD, *holding a shield and spear.* DAEDALUS *and* KING MINOS *stand downstage, talking.* ICARUS *roams around the stage.*

From time to time, he stops to pick up and study a seashell. THE CHORUS MEMBERS *are lined up in front of the rock at stage left. Before speaking, each* CHORUS MEMBER *takes a step forward. After speaking, he or she steps back in line.*

- Everybody, how long ago does the play take place? (Signal.) *Over 2 thousand years ago.*
- Where does act 1 take place? (Call on a student. Idea: *On a beach in Crete; in front of a maze.*)
- Crete is an island near Greece.
4. Follow along while I read the first part of the play.

CHORUS MEMBER 1:

(Pointing to DAEDALUS*)*

Daedalus is a famous artist, inventor, and builder. He is known throughout the land for the clever things he creates. His statues are so lifelike they seem to breathe. His palaces are so magnificent, they rival those of the gods on Mount Olympus. His fame has reached even to the island of Crete.

- The people who lived on the island of Crete back then thought that there were many gods, and that the gods lived on top of a magical mountain called Mount Olympus.
- What are some of the things that Daedalus has built? (Call on a student. Ideas: *Statues, palaces.*)
5. Follow along while I read.

CHORUS MEMBER 2:

(Pointing to KING MINOS*)*

King Minos, who rules Crete, is a tyrant—a cruel and wicked man. He offered Daedalus a great deal of money to build a prison for a horrible beast called the *Minotaur.* The Minotaur has the body of a man and the head of a bull. For years, he has terrified the people of Crete. But the Minotaur is also the son of King Minos' wife, and so the king does not want to kill him. Daedalus accepted King Minos' offer.

(Pointing to the walled maze)

To hold the Minotaur, he has built this splendid maze, called the *Labyrinth.* The soldiers are getting ready to bring the Minotaur to the Labyrinth.

- Everybody, who asked Daedalus to come to Crete? (Signal.) *King Minos.*
- What was Daedalus supposed to build for the king? (Call on a student. Ideas: *A labyrinth; a maze.*)
- What creature would be placed in the Labyrinth? (Signal.) *The Minotaur.*
- Why didn't the king want to kill the Minotaur? (Call on a student. Idea: *Because the Minotaur is the son of the king's wife.*)

6. Follow along.

> **DAEDALUS:**
> *(To* KING MINOS*)*
>
> My Labyrinth has hundreds of twisted and tangled paths. Anyone who enters it soon becomes hopelessly lost. Once inside, the Minotaur can never escape. Indeed, only *I* know how to find the way out.

- Everybody, who is the only one that knows the way out of the Labyrinth? (Signal.) *Daedalus.*

7. Follow along.

> **KING MINOS:**
> *(With impatience)*
>
> Yes, yes. So you have said before.
>
> **DAEDALUS:**
>
> If you doubt me, ask your soldiers who have tried to solve the puzzle. If I had not saved them, they would all still be inside the Labyrinth.
>
> **CHORUS MEMBER 3:**
> *(Pointing to* ICARUS*)*
>
> When Daedalus came to Crete, he brought along his son, Icarus. Icarus is brave and smart, but he often acts and speaks without thinking.
>
> ICARUS *reaches the entrance to the maze. He glances at his father, then starts to go inside.*
>
> **DAEDALUS:**
>
> Icarus! No! How many times have I told you that you must never go inside the Labyrinth! Remember the soldiers?
>
> **ICARUS:**
> *(Laughing)*
>
> Oh, Father! I am much smarter than a common soldier. I'm sure that I can find my way through your maze.
>
> **DAEDALUS:**
>
> If you were truly smart, you would learn to listen to those who are older and wiser.
>
> ICARUS *skips to his father's side. An angry roar fills the air. The* GUARDS *tremble, their spears rattling against their shields. The* CHORUS MEMBERS *scramble behind the rock.*

DAEDALUS:
(Pulling ICARUS *near)*

> The Minotaur!

KING MINOS:

> Of course. You say that the beast can never escape from this Labyrinth, but as yet I have seen no proof of your claim.

(Turning toward the GUARDS*)*

> Bring the Minotaur here!

The GUARDS *exit, still trembling. From offstage, the roars become louder and angrier. They are mixed with the shouts and cries of the* GUARDS:

FIRST GUARD:

> Move him this way! Quickly! No, don't let him turn!

SECOND GUARD:

> Yes! Yes! I know. Watch him! Watch him!

The MINOTAUR *enters, roaring and stomping. His hands are tied behind his back.* KING MINOS *and* DAEDALUS *take a few steps backward.* ICARUS *remains where he is, watching the action with excitement.*

DAEDALUS:
(Grabbing his son's robe and tugging him backward)

> Icarus!

ICARUS:

> I want to help!

The GUARDS *dance around the* MINOTAUR, *lunging at him with their spears. They force him inside the Labyrinth, and he turns and disappears down a pathway. As the* MINOTAUR'S *roars become more and more faint, everyone on stage breathes deeply. The* CHORUS MEMBERS *come out from behind the rock and line up once more. The* GUARDS *take their positions.* ICARUS *runs to the entrance and peeks inside.*

CHORUS MEMBER 1:

> And so the Minotaur was trapped in the Labyrinth. With this, Daedalus thought his work was finished.

CHORUS MEMBER 2:

> But remember, King Minos is a wicked man. He cannot be trusted.

DAEDALUS:

Come, Icarus, it is time for us to say good-bye to King Minos. We must prepare to sail for home.

KING MINOS:
(Smiling slyly)

I regret that your plans will have to change. As you have told me, you are the only person who knows how to escape from the Labyrinth. Do you really think that I can let you leave this island with such valuable knowledge? What if my enemies find out the secret? What if they release the Minotaur? Oh, no. I cannot risk that.

(Motioning to the GUARDS*)*

Come, take these two to the tower and lock them up!

The GUARDS *start toward* DAEDALUS *and* ICARUS. ICARUS *charges them, swinging his fists. The first* GUARD *smiles and takes* ICARUS *firmly by the arm. The second* GUARD *points a spear at* DAEDALUS.

- Why wouldn't the king let Daedalus leave Crete? (Call on a student. Idea: *Because Daedalus knows how to get out of the Labyrinth.*)
- Why didn't the king just put Daedalus and Icarus in the Labyrinth? (Call on a student. Idea: *Because Daedalus knows how to get out.*)
- Where did the king tell the guards to take them? (Call on a student. Idea: *To the tower.*)
8. Follow along.

DAEDALUS:

Icarus! Do as they say.

ICARUS:

But, Father . . . !

The GUARDS *march their prisoners offstage.*

CHORUS MEMBER 3:

Poor Daedalus! Poor Icarus! What will happen to them now?

The lights dim.

ACT 2

Time:
A year later.

Setting:
Inside a gloomy high tower on the coast of Crete. DAEDALUS *sits on a wooden bench, head in hands.* ICARUS *stands beside a large window.*

Through the window, several seabirds can be seen soaring through the air. The Chorus Members *stand in shadows downstage.*

- Everybody, when does Act 2 take place? (Signal.) *A year later.*
- Where does it take place? (Call on a student. Idea: *In the tower where Daedalus and Icarus are.*)
- Who is in this act besides the chorus? (Call on a student.) *Daedalus and Icarus.*
9. Follow along.

Chorus Member 1:

King Minos has made Daedalus and Icarus prisoners in this high tower near the sea. They have only a pile of straw to sleep on. Their only visitors are the guards who bring them food.

Chorus Member 2:

At first, Daedalus did not worry. After all, he was known far and wide for his cleverness. He was sure that he could find a way to escape the tower. Alas, all of his clever plans for escape have failed, and failure has made him very unhappy.

(Pointing to Daedalus*)*

He has given up hope.

Chorus Member 3:
(Pointing to Icarus*)*

But Icarus has not given up hope for escape. Each day he stands at the window and watches for ships.

Icarus:
(Turning to Daedalus*)*

Come, look, Father! There is a ship far away on the horizon. Perhaps we can signal it.

Daedalus:
(Looking at his son with a sad smile)

With what, my son? We cannot make a fire. We have no cloth to wave. And you know that King Minos has promised death to anyone who helps us to escape. What ship's captain or crew will defy the king?

Icarus:
(Sighing)

You are right, Father. We can never leave this place.

(He turns back to watch the birds.)

But at least come watch the beautiful birds. They move so easily through the sky.

DAEDALUS:

(Walking to the window)

>Yes, they are beautiful.

*(He watches for a moment,
then claps his hands and laughs.)*

>Of course! I've been blind! Thank you, my son, for opening my eyes. King Minos may block us from leaving by sea, but he does not control the sky.

(Slapping ICARUS on the back)

>We will fly out of this prison!

ICARUS:

>Oh, Father, how can we fly? We are not birds.

DAEDALUS:

>We are not birds, but we can fly! You will see!

The stage goes dark. A spotlight focuses on the CHORUS MEMBERS.

CHORUS MEMBER 1:

>Daedalus began to place bits of bread from their meals on the windowsill. Soon the birds were flocking to the window and fighting among themselves for the bread. As they squabbled, feathers flew everywhere, and Icarus hurried to collect as many as possible.

CHORUS MEMBER 2:

>Daedalus showed Icarus how to arrange the feathers in order of size. Using a needle he made from a piece of bone and thread taken from his robe, he sewed together the feathers, shaping them into wings. He used leather from his belt and sandals to make straps and harnesses, and he attached the wings to the harnesses with candle wax.

CHORUS MEMBER 3:

>Then one day at sunrise, Daedalus woke Icarus.

The stage lightens. ICARUS *is asleep on the pile of straw.* DAEDALUS *is standing nearby. He is wearing one pair of wings and holding a smaller pair.*

DAEDALUS:

>Come my son, your wings are ready. Let me help you put them on.

ICARUS *gets up, rubbing the sleep from his eyes. He stands as* DAEDALUS *slips the wings over his arms.*

ICARUS:

I'm afraid, Father. I don't know how to make the wings work.

DAEDALUS:

First, spread them like this.

(Spreading his arms and wings wide)

Then slowly move them up and down.

ICARUS:

(Flapping his wings and moving around the stage, slowly at first, then faster and faster)

Look at me! I'm flying! I'm flying. Let's leave now!

(He starts for the tower window.)

DAEDALUS:

No, not yet. Before we leave, you must listen closely to what I tell you.

ICARUS:

(Dropping his wings to his sides)

Yes, Father, I will listen.

DAEDALUS:

Good, because your life depends on doing as I say. You must stay close to me. If you fly too low, the sea water will make your feathers heavy, and you will sink into the water. If you fly too high, the sun will melt the candle wax and your wings will fall off. Do you understand?

ICARUS:

I understand, Father.

DAEDALUS:

Then let us fly before the guards come with our food.

They flap their wings and circle around the stage several times, then each goes to the window and leaps out.

DAEDALUS:

(Offstage)

Remember, stay close to me and do what I said.

ICARUS:

(Offstage)

      Yes, Father. I'm flying! I'm flying!

The lights dim.

ACT 2

Time:
Minutes later.

Setting:
A backdrop shows both pale blue sky with clouds and bright sun and a deep blue sea with foamy waves. DAEDALUS and ICARUS circle around the stage, flapping their wings. The CHORUS MEMBERS stand at stage left.

- How much later does this act take place? (Call on a student. Idea: *Minutes later.*)
- What is the setting for this act? (Call on a student. Idea: *On the beach.*)

10. Follow along.

CHORUS MEMBER 1:

      And so Daedalus and Icarus have escaped from the tower.

CHORUS MEMBER 2:

      At first, Icarus does as his father has told him.

CHORUS MEMBER 3:

      But the joy of flying soon makes Icarus forget his father's warnings. Before long, he is swooping close to the water and soaring high in the sky.

ICARUS:

      Try this, Father!
(Bending toward the sea)
      And this!
(Leaping toward the sun)

DAEDALUS:

      Icarus! Stop that! This is not a game!
(ICARUS gets closer and closer to the sun.)
      What are you doing? Come back!

ICARUS:
*(Stopping suddenly. For a moment,
he stands with his wings outstretched.
Then the wings begin to slip from his arms.)*

Father! The wax is melting! I'm falling!

ICARUS *sinks slowly to the floor.* DAEDALUS, *flapping his wings, circles him.*

DAEDALUS:

My son! My son!

The lights dim, then the stage goes dark. A spotlight shows the CHORUS MEMBERS.

CHORUS MEMBER 1:

Icarus disappeared into the dark sea.

CHORUS MEMBER 2:

Daedalus searched and searched for his son, but all he found were feathers floating on the water. Weeping bitter tears, he flew on until he reached land.

CHORUS MEMBER 3:

There he built a temple to Apollo, the Greek god of youth and life. And on the walls of the temple, Daedalus placed his wings, never to fly again.

Curtain closes.

The End

- Daedalus built a temple to which god? (Call on a student. Ideas: *Apollo; god of youth and life.*)
- Why do you think he built the temple to the god of youth and life? (Call on a student. Idea: *Because he missed his son.*)
- What did he do with his wings? (Call on a student. Idea: *Put them on the temple wall.*)
- How many times did he use his wings after that day? (Call on a student. Idea: *Never.*)
11. This time, I'll call on individual students to read parts of the play.
    (Call on individual students to read the whole play at least one more time.)
12. This time, we'll have individual students read the characters' parts. (Assign good readers to be the chorus members, Daedalus, and King Minos. Assign other students for the remaining roles.)

Activity

1. (Direct and assist students in making or gathering modest props, stage settings, and costumes.)
2. (Put on a reading version of the play for another group of students.)

Literary Preferences—Part 1

1. (Make copies of blackline masters 15A and 15B.)
- (Distribute copies of blackline masters to students.)
2. You've read stories by different authors. You're going to compare authors to see which ones you like the most. Those are the ones you would choose to read on your own.
3. Find part A on your worksheet. ✔
- You're going to pick the three stories in your anthology that you liked the best. Start by reading the titles and the authors. Find the selection you liked the best and write the number **1** next to it. Write the number in the column titled **Rank.** The number-one ranking is the highest ranking.
  (Observe students and give feedback.)
4. Now find the selection you liked next best and write the number **2** next to it.
  (Observe students and give feedback.)
5. Now find the selection you liked next best and write the number **3** next to it.
6. I'll read each title. Raise your hand if you wrote **1, 2,** or **3** next to the title.
- The *Velveteen Rabbit* by Harriet Winfield. Raise your hand if you wrote a number next to that title.
- (Count raised hands. Write the total on your copy of the worksheet in the **Rank** column.)
- (Repeat for the remaining titles.)
7. (On your copy of the worksheet, circle the three titles with the highest numbers.)
- (Write on the board:)

Title	Author

- (Write the titles and authors of the three most frequently selected titles. Write the titles in rank order, with the most frequently selected title first.)
- Here are the three favorite titles and authors for the group.

Literary Preferences—Part 2

1. Find part B on your worksheet. ✔
- You're going to write about your number-one selection. Write the title and author of your favorite selection in the blanks at the top of part B.
  (Observe students and give feedback.)
2. Find the heading **plot.** ✔
- Listen: The **plot** is the story itself—what happens to the characters in the story. The plot doesn't tell about the words the author used, how clear the author was, or whether the author wrote simple sentences or more difficult sentences.
- Write what you liked about the story plot of your number-one selection. Tell whether you liked this plot better than any of the others we have read. Tell why. (Observe students and give feedback.)

3. Find the heading **style.** ✔

- The **style** has to do with the kind of sentences the author wrote and the words that the author used. If the author writes very long sentences, that's part of the author's style. If the author writes things that are funny, that's part of the author's style. If the author often writes about how things look or sound, that's part of the author's style.

- Write some things you liked about the style of your number-one author. Maybe you liked the way the author described things so you could really picture them. Maybe you liked the kind of sentences that the author used. Maybe they were short and clear; maybe they were long, but interesting; maybe the words themselves sounded pleasant or musical.

  (Observe students and give feedback.)

4. Find the heading **theme.** ✔

- Remember, the **theme** is the lesson the story teaches. If a story shows that it's not a good idea to trust strangers, that would be a theme. The plot of the story tells about the characters and what happens to them. Stories that have the **same theme** may have **different** characters and **different** things may happen.

- Write what you liked about the theme of your number-one story. If you're not sure of the theme, tell what kind of story you would like the author of your favorite story to write. Would you like to know more about one of the characters? Would you like to read another story that had the same kind of plot? Write several sentences that tell about that story you would like to read.

5. (Call on individual students to read their evaluations of the plot, the author's style, and the theme.)

Title	Author	Rank
The Velveteen Rabbit	Harriet Winfield	
Dreams	Langston Hughes	
The Runner	Faustin Charles	
The Emperor's New Clothes	Harvey Cleaver	
Why Leopard Has Black Spots	Told by Won-Ldy Paye	
Boar Out There	Cynthia Rylant	
Crossing the Creek	Laura Ingalls Wilder	
Camp on the High Prairie	Laura Ingalls Wilder	
Spaghetti	Cynthia Rylant	
Charlie Best	Ruth Corrin	
The Pancake Collector	Jack Prelutsky	
Not Just Any Ring	Danita Ross Haller	
A Lucky Thing	Alice Schertle	
The New Kid	Mike Makley	
Steps	Deborah M. Newton Chocolate	
The Soup Stone	Retold by Maria Leach	
Julie Rescues Big Mack	Roger Hall	
Amelia Bedelia	Peggy Parish	
My (Wow!) Summer Vacation	Susan Cornell Poskanzer	
The Story of Daedalus and Icarus	Fran Lehr	

B

My number-one selection is _____ .

It was written by _____ .

1. Plot

_____

_____

_____

_____

2. Style

_____

_____

_____

_____

3. Theme

_____

_____

_____

_____

Supplementary Novels

Two supplementary novels are recommended for independent student reading after the students have completed lesson 140. The novels are
- *The Chalk Box Kid*—Clyde Robert Bulla
- *Pirate Island Adventure*—Peggy Parish

Here are the procedures for introducing the novels.

Obtain enough copies of each novel. Both novels are available through school and public libraries. You can also order the novels from a paperback book club. If you order the novels through a paperback book club, make sure you place your order at least two months before the novels will be needed.

Assemble the students in the group. Make and distribute copies of the blackline masters for the novel.

Read the word lists for section 1 aloud. Each novel has been divided into sections, and each section has its own word list and questions. Read the word list for section 1 aloud as the students follow along. Then have the students read the word list for section 1. Discuss the meaning of the words marked with an asterisk*. (For words that have more than one meaning, check the story for the appropriate meaning.) Then have the students orally read the questions for section 1.

Structure the reading of the first two or three pages of the novel. These pages typically contain vocabulary and sentence forms that may be new to the students. Call on individual students to read several sentences in turn. Explain any words or sentences that the students do not understand.

Have the students read the rest of section 1 to themselves. A good procedure is to put a paper clip on the last page of section 1 so that the students know to stop there. After the students finish reading section 1, they must answer the questions for section 1. Correct their answers using the answer keys on pages 138–141.

Follow a similar procedure for each remaining section of the novel. However, the students do not have to read any of the remaining sections aloud.

After the students complete the novel and the questions, you may want to have them write a book report on the novel. If possible, post the reports or have the students read them aloud.

Book 1: The Chalk Box Kid
Section 1 (Chapters 1–4)

1

sofa
tablet
factory*
Gregory
Aunt Grace

2

Perry
Vance
bragging
loose
bricks

3

porch
uncle
guitar
thumbtacks*
paintbrush
concrete*

4

Ivy
shy*
castle
plink
alligator

B Write answers to these questions on lined paper.

1. What were Gregory's parents doing while he stayed with Aunt Grace?

2. Whose birthday was it?

3. Gregory got something for his birthday that was better than a cake or a party. What was it?

4. Did Gregory's new house have a yard?

5. The first morning in his new house, Gregory painted several pictures. What pictures did he paint?

6. What did he do with the pictures?

7. Uncle Max called Gregory the ▇▇▇ Kid.

8. What did Gregory tell Miss Perry about North Lake School?

9. Who said that Gregory was wrong about North Lake School?

10. What did Uncle Max do that made Gregory angry?

11. Where did Gregory go after he got angry at Uncle Max?

12. Why was Uncle Max staying with Gregory's family?

13. Whose room did Uncle Max share?

14. What was unusual about how Ivy talked?

15. Why did she talk that way?

16. Where did Gregory go after school every day?

17. Why didn't his mother want him to go there?

18. What did the burned building used to be?

19. What did Gregory do to the walls of the burned building?

20. What did he use?

Section 2 (Chapters 5–9)

1

blackboard
sunflowers*
strawberries
afterward
anytime

2

radishes
sweet peas*
vegetables
cream
walnut

3

grand prize*
blue ribbon*
Cartright
Mr. Hiller
nursery
lettuce

4

pear
fountain
chocolate
dessert
Richard

B **Write answers to these questions on lined paper.**

1. During Gregory's second week at school, there was a party. Who was the party for?

2. Why was there a party?

3. What special prize was given at the party?

4. Where did Mr. Hiller work?

5. What did he bring for the students in the class?

6. Did Gregory plant a garden?

7. Tell why.

8. Where was Gregory's garden?

9. It rained one night. What did Gregory worry about?

10. Why was Gregory almost late to school the next morning?

11. Which student asked Gregory about his garden?

12. What did that student want to know?

13. Who were the first people to see Gregory's garden?

14. What did Vance say about Gregory's garden?

15. How did that make Gregory feel?

16. How do you know?

17. What did Ivy bring to school?

18. Who did she give it to?

19. Why did she give it to that person?

20. Who wanted to take a picture of Gregory's garden?

21. What did that person do with the picture?

22. After Uncle Max saw Gregory's garden, he called Gregory the ▮▮▮▮ Kid.

23. What did Uncle Max do with his posters?

24. How were the kids at school different?

25. Who came to visit Gregory at the end of the story?

26. How did that make Gregory feel?

Book 2: Pirate Island Adventure
Section 1 (Chapters 1 and 2)

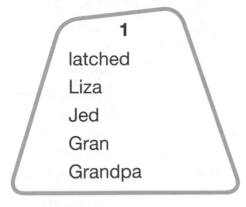

1
latched
Liza
Jed
Gran
Grandpa

2
mystery
miracles*
gaggle of geese*
Fergusons
arrangements*

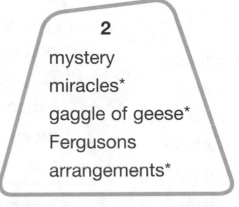

3
include
caretaker*
hurray
squabbling*
gee
spur-of-the-moment*

4
married
eagerly
college
busiest
support a family*

B Write answers to these questions on lined paper.

1. Where did Gran and Grandpa plan to take the children for the summer?

2. Had the children ever been there?

3. What was Jelly Bean?

4. What did the children do while they waited for their father to get home?

5. Grandpa didn't want Dad to tell the children any stories about the island. Why not?

6. Who was the oldest child in the family?

7. Who owned the house on Pirate Island?

8. Who had been taking care of the house?

9. Why couldn't those people continue caring for the house?

A

1

Mainland
anyway
grandchildren
motorboat
outnumbered*
driveway

2

grandparents
proceed*
schedule*
lemonade
runaways
plane reservations*

3

islanders
old-timers*
boat taxi*
inconvenient*
primitive*
fads*

4

ourselves
volunteer*
yippee
hectic*
due to arrive*

5

dare
celebration*
potato
resort*
steal someone's thunder

6

yep
committee*
snuggled
contentedly*
grumbled

B **Write answers to these questions on lined paper.**

1. Who came up with the idea to fly to Pirate Island?

2. Who had to be talked into flying?

3. Were there stores on Pirate Island?

4. How did people on the island get groceries?

5. About how many people lived on Pirate Island all the time?

6. Why didn't Gran and Grandpa live on Pirate Island all the time?

7. Who was always ready to eat—Jed, Liza or Bill?

8. Grandpa gave the children a picture clue for a new mystery. What was the picture?

Section 3 (Chapters 5 and 6)

A

1

needlepoint*
silversmith*
whoever
grandfather
sprawled*
memories

2

particular*
razor blade
embroidery*
sewing
initials
occasion

5

naughty
code*
scraggly*
accepted
in bloom*

3

wedding
scurrying*
yapping
squirmed
treeing*
luggage

4

fascinated*
coffee
flight number*
aloft*
goodness
annoyed*

6

drone*
according
transferred*
hired
chaos*

B **Write answers to these questions on lined paper.**

1. Grandpa's brother hid something that belonged to each member of his family. What belonged to Grandpa?

2. What belonged to Grandpa's sister?

3. What belonged to Grandpa's mother?

4. What belonged to Grandpa's father?

5. Why didn't Grandpa's family look for their treasures the next summer?

6. What did Grandpa know about the bush in the picture clue?

7. Did he know if it was still there?

8. Tell why.

9. Where was Jelly Bean when the family was ready to leave for the airport?

10. What was he doing?

11. The children didn't eat much breakfast before they left for the airport. Why not?

12. Who was nervous about flying?

13. Did they enjoy the trip?

14. What did they do on the plane?

15. How did the family get from Mainland to Pirate Island?

16. What was the first task they had to do when they got to the island?

Section 4 (Chapters 7 and 8)

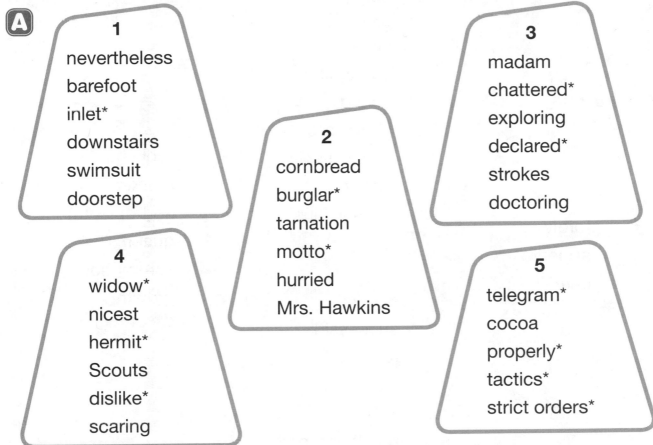

A

1
nevertheless
barefoot
inlet*
downstairs
swimsuit
doorstep

2
cornbread
burglar*
tarnation
motto*
hurried
Mrs. Hawkins

3
madam
chattered*
exploring
declared*
strokes
doctoring

4
widow*
nicest
hermit*
Scouts
dislike*
scaring

5
telegram*
cocoa
properly*
tactics*
strict orders*

B **Write answers to these questions on lined paper.**

1. Why did the family think someone was in their house when they arrived on the island?
2. Who was in the house?
3. What was she doing?
4. What task did Gran want the children to do after they ate Mrs. Hawkins's snack?
5. What did they do when they finished that task?
6. Gran didn't want the children to go barefoot. Why not?
7. Where did the family go swimming?
8. Who gave the children a swimming lesson?
9. What was in the package that the family found on the doorstep?
10. Who left the package?
11. Why did Hermit Dan try to scare the summer people?
12. What was Liza, Jed and Bill's last name?

Section 5 (Chapters 9 and 10)

A

1

early bird*
shared
awake
forgiven
appetite*
cereal

2

in a jiffy*
straggled
gang
hopeless*
necessarily
crummy
suspicious*

3

tool shed*
market
sort objects*
queer
scrumptious*
growth

4

known
successful
recipe*
rightly
in bud*
private property*

B **Write answers to these questions on lined paper.**

1. The first morning on the island, who was the first child to wake up?
2. Who had already gone swimming?
3. What did the children decide to look for after breakfast?
4. What did they ask Grandpa before they went looking?
5. Did they take the picture clue with them?
6. Tell why.
7. Did the children find the bush the first time they looked for it?
8. What did they decide Liza should do?
9. What did Liza ask Grandpa about the bush?
10. What was his answer?
11. Grandpa said the bush was queer. Name one thing that was queer about it.
12. Who found the right bush?
13. Why did the children need tools at the end of chapter 10?

Section 6 (Chapters 11 and 12)

A

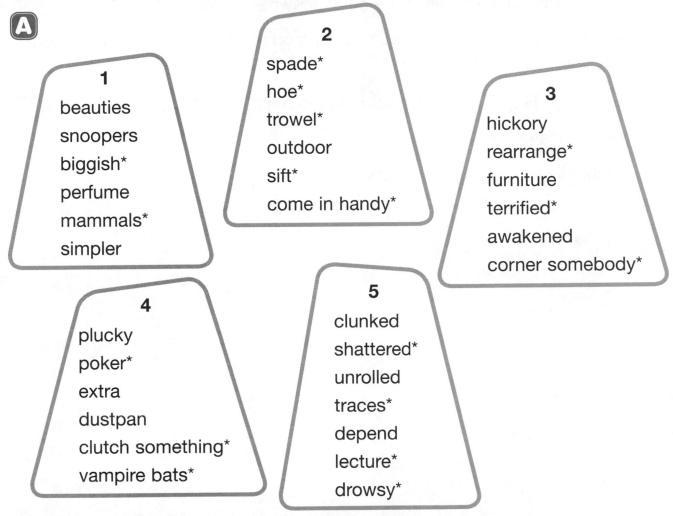

1
beauties
snoopers
biggish*
perfume
mammals*
simpler

2
spade*
hoe*
trowel*
outdoor
sift*
come in handy*

3
hickory
rearrange*
furniture
terrified*
awakened
corner somebody*

4
plucky
poker*
extra
dustpan
clutch something*
vampire bats*

5
clunked
shattered*
unrolled
traces*
depend
lecture*
drowsy*

B **Write answers to these questions on lined paper.**

1. Grandpa didn't want to show the children where his favorite fishing spot was. Why not?

2. What did Grandpa teach the children to do in chapter 11?

3. What digging tools did the children find?

4. How many dashes were on the picture clue?

5. What did each dash stand for?

6. Why was Bill chosen to count the number of steps from the bush?

7. How did the children break the jar they found?

8. What picture clue was inside the jar?

9. Why did the children fill in the holes they had dug?

10. The children didn't get to start working on the second picture clue right away. Why not?

11. Why was Jelly Bean barking during the night?

12. Do bats lay eggs?

13. What class of animals are bats in?

Section 7 (Chapters 13 and 14)

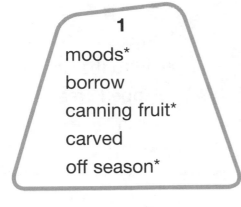

1

moods*
borrow
canning fruit*
carved
off season*

2

trust
frame house*
gracious
make a living*
punched

3

clonked
flock*
knot
pension*

4

garden plot*
chickens
scowl*
oddball

B Write answers to these questions on lined paper.

1. Jed looked at the picture clue through a magnifying glass. What did he notice?

2. What did Liza notice?

3. Who got more information from Grandpa about the heart tree?

4. Who had carved the heart on the heart tree?

5. Whose initials were in the heart?

6. How did Gran feel the first time she saw the carved heart?

7. Who was Jed named after?

8. Who found the "x" on the picture clue of the tree?

9. Where was the "x" on the tree?

10. Why were the children planning to help with lunch?

11. Why didn't they help with lunch?

12. How did the islanders earn extra money?

13. Name 3 things Hermit Dan did for the islanders.

Section 8 (Chapters 15 and 16)

A

1
situation*
bless
set in your ways*
trapped
strawberry shortcake

2
sorriest
tend to the dog*
whipped cream
foolish*
awed*

3
chasing
skunk
lavender soap*
backside
shoo
stop in your tracks*

4
carvings
disclose*
boosted
furry
raccoon*

B **Write answers to these questions on lined paper.**

1. What did the family have for dessert at Mrs. Hawkins's house?

2. Who supplies Mrs. Hawkins with a lot of her food?

3. The title of chapter 15 was "Jelly Bean Trouble." What trouble did Jelly Bean get into?

4. How did Liza get skunk smell on her?

5. How did the children try to get the smell off Jelly Bean?

6. The children went exploring in the woods. Who did they hide from?

7. What was that person looking for?

8. Why was that person mad?

9. The hole in the initial tree was much higher than it seemed to be in the picture clue. Why?

10. Why did Liza scream when she stuck her hand into the hole?

11. At the end of chapter 16, the children decided to return to the tree after dark. How would that solve their problem?

Section 9 (Chapters 17 and 18)

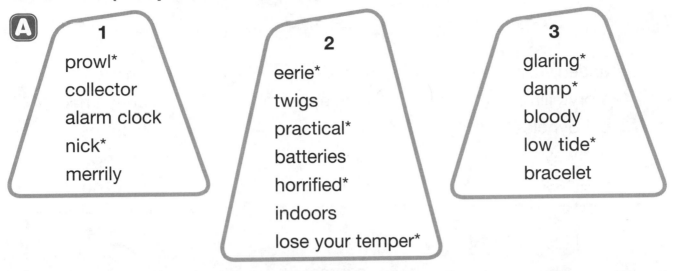

A

1
prowl*
collector
alarm clock
nick*
merrily

2
eerie*
twigs
practical*
batteries
horrified*
indoors
lose your temper*

3
glaring*
damp*
bloody
low tide*
bracelet

B Write answers to these questions on lined paper.

1. Which child was interested in seashells?

2. What did Grandpa find for that child?

3. What did Jed do to make sure he woke up for the trip to the woods?

4. About what time was it when the children headed into the woods?

5. When the children headed into the woods, each child had a flashlight. What happened to Liza's flashlight?

6. What happened to Bill's flashlight?

7. What happened to Jed's flashlight?

8. Bill found something in the tree hole after he cleaned out the bark and twigs. What did he find?

9. Why did Jed dig a hole near the tree?

10. Why didn't the children study the new clue when they got back to the house from the woods?

11. Liza explained that Jed and Bill got into a fight because they wanted to do different things. What did Jed want to do?

12. What did Bill want to do?

13. What did Bill do that made Jed so angry?

Section 10 (Chapters 19 and 20)

A

1
underbrush*
storytelling
cubbyholes*
partway
endless*

2
rusted
yourselves
natural*
accident
evidence*

3
busily
concerned
thermos*
hoeing
gurgling

4
source*
delicious
poking
obvious*
attic

B **Write answers to these questions on lined paper.**

1. What did the third picture clue show?

2. Why didn't Grandpa want to tell the children exactly where the cave was?

3. Grandpa gave the children a clue about where the cave was. He said the cave was right by ███.

4. What did the children find on their way to the stream and the cave?

5. How did the children use sticks in the cave?

6. What did Jed find in one of the cubbyholes?

7. Why couldn't the children get it open at first?

8. The fourth picture clue was in two parts. What did the first part show?

Section 11 (Chapters 21 and 22)

A

1
fisherman
drawstring*
floorboard
someplace
tag along*

2
lantern*
squiggles
contraption*
further
jut out*
chain links*

3
be patient*
by invitation*
squirmy
off-limits*
tissue*

4
tarnish*
collection
gorgeous*
polished
grand-niece*

B **Write answers to these questions on lined paper.**

1. Why hadn't the children ever noticed the round window on the front of the house?

2. What did the children find out from Grandpa that helped them with the last picture clue?

3. Both grandparents left the house while the children explored the attic. Where did Gran go?

4. Where did Grandpa go?

5. Why did Jed pound on the attic wall with a hammer?

6. Whose secret room did the children find?

7. Why did that person have a secret room?

8. Had Grandpa ever been in the secret room?

9. Each child got one of the treasures from the secret room. What did Jed get?

10. What did Liza get?

11. What did Bill get?

Answer Key

The Chalk Box Kid

SECTION 1

1. *Idea:* Moving to a new house
2. Gregory's
3. *Idea:* A room of his own
4. No
5. A house and a sunflower
6. *Idea:* Put them up on his bedroom wall
7. Paintbrush
8. *Idea:* That it was bigger than Dover Street School
9. Vance
10. *Idea:* Uncle Max put his posters over Gregory's pictures.
11. *Idea:* To the burned building behind his house
12. *Ideas:* Because he didn't have a job; he needed a place to stay.
13. Gregory's
14. *Idea:* She talked very softly.
15. *Idea:* Because she was shy
16. *Idea:* To the burned building behind his house
17. *Idea:* Because it was so dirty
18. A chalk factory
19. *Idea:* He drew pictures on the walls.
20. Chalk

SECTION 2

1. Ivy
2. *Idea:* Because Ivy had won the grand prize in an art show
3. *Idea:* A case filled with paints, brushes, pens and pencils
4. *Idea:* At a nursery
5. Plants and seeds
6. No
7. *Idea:* Because he didn't have a place for one
8. *Idea:* In the chalk factory
9. *Idea:* That his drawings would be washed away
10. *Idea:* Because he had been working in his garden
11. Vance
12. *Idea:* Where Gregory's garden was
13. *Idea:* Some students from Gregory's class
14. *Idea:* That it was nothing at all.
15. *Ideas:* Upset; hurt; angry
16. *Ideas:* Because he wasn't hungry that night; because he didn't eat dessert that night
17. *Idea:* Her case of art supplies
18. Gregory
19. *Idea:* Because she thought his pictures were better than hers
20. Mr. Hiller
21. *Idea:* Put it up at his nursery
22. Chalk Box
23. *Idea:* He took them down.
24. *Idea:* They were more friendly.
25. *Idea:* Ivy and her little brother
26. *Idea:* Happy

Answer Key

Pirate Island Adventure

SECTION 1

1. To Pirate Island
2. No
3. *Idea:* A dog
4. *Idea:* Studied
5. *Idea:* He wanted to tell the stories himself.
6. Jed
7. Gran and Grandpa
8. *Idea:* The Fergusons
9. *Idea:* Because Mr. Ferguson died

SECTION 2

1. *Idea:* The children's mother
2. Grandpa
3. a. No
4. *Idea:* A motorboat delivered them.
5. *Idea:* A dozen
6. *Idea:* Because they wanted to be closer to their children and grandchildren
7. Bill
8. *Idea:* A bush with red flowers and some broken lines

SECTION 3

1. *Idea:* A ship model
2. *Idea:* A needlepoint bag
3. *Idea:* A silver pin
4. *Idea:* A silver belt buckle
5. *Idea:* They didn't go back to the island the next summer.
6. *Idea:* It was in back of the house.
7. No
8. *Ideas:* He wouldn't recognize it without the flowers; it hadn't been in bloom when he and Gran had been there.
9. *Idea:* In the backyard
10. *Ideas:* Treeing the kittens; barking at the kittens
11. *Idea:* They were too excited.
12. Gran and Grandpa
13. Yes
14. *Idea:* Looked out the window
15. *Idea:* By boat taxi
16. *Idea:* Carry the baggage to the house

SECTION 4

1. *Idea:* Because they could smell coffee and bread
2. Mrs. Hawkins
3. *Idea:* Making a snack for the family
4. *Idea:* Unpack
5. *Idea:* Went swimming
6. *Ideas:* They might cut their feet; there were lots of broken seashells around.
7. *Idea:* At the inlet
8. Gran
9. Fish
10. Hermit Dan
11. *Idea:* So they would leave him alone
12. Roberts

SECTION 5

1. Bill
2. Gran and Grandpa
3. *Idea:* The bush from the picture clue
4. *Idea:* Which side of the yard the bush was on
5. No
6. *Idea:* They wanted to keep it safe.
7. No
8. *Idea:* Find out more about the bush from Grandpa
9. *Idea:* When it would bloom
10. *Ideas:* Soon; anytime now
11. *Ideas:* The flowers came out before the leaves; it never got over three feet high.
12. Liza
13. *Idea:* To dig around the bush

SECTION 6

1. *Idea:* He wanted them to find it for themselves.
2. *Idea:* Clean fish
3. Spades and a trowel
4. 10
5. *Idea:* One step
6. *Idea:* He had the biggest feet.
7. *Idea:* They dropped a rock on it.
8. *Idea:* A tree
9. *Idea:* So no one would know they'd been digging
10. *Idea:* Because Gran and Grandpa wanted help moving furniture
11. *Idea:* Because there was a bat in the house
12. No
13. Mammals

SECTION 7

1. *Idea:* There were letters on the tree.
2. *Idea:* There was a heart on the tree.
3. Liza
4. *Idea:* Great-Uncle John
5. Gran and Grandpa's
6. *Idea:* Embarrassed
7. *Idea:* Great-Uncle John
8. Bill
9. *Idea:* In the middle of the hole
10. *Idea:* So they could get away sooner
11. *Idea:* Because they went to Mrs. Hawkins's for lunch
12. *Idea:* By taking care of the resort houses
13. *Ideas:* Catches fish; leaves fresh eggs; gathers fruit; grows vegetables

SECTION 8

1. Strawberry shortcake
2. Hermit Dan
3. *Idea:* He got sprayed by a skunk.
4. *Idea:* She picked up Jelly Bean.
5. *Idea:* They washed him in the stream.
6. Hermit Dan
7. A skunk had a raccoon.
8. *Idea:* Because something got in his corn the night before
9. *Idea:* Because the tree had grown since the picture clue was drawn
10. *Idea:* Because there was a raccoon in the hole
11. *Idea:* The raccoon would be out hunting.

SECTION 9

1. Jed
2. *Idea:* An old book about seashells
3. *Idea:* He set an alarm clock.
4. Midnight
5. *Idea:* The batteries were dead.
6. *Idea:* He lost it.
7. *Idea:* It broke when Bill fell with it.
8. *Idea:* A jar
9. *Idea:* To bury the broken jar
10. *Ideas:* They were too tired; they were cold and damp.
11. *Idea:* Read about the seashell he had found
12. *Idea:* Study the new clue
13. *Idea:* Broke Jed's new seashell

SECTION 10

1. *Idea:* Some woods, a stream and a cave
2. *Idea:* He wanted them to find it on their own.
3. *Idea:* His fishing spot
4. *Idea:* Hermit Dan's garden
5. *Idea:* They poked the sticks into the cubbyholes.
6. *Idea:* A box
7. *Idea:* It was rusted shut.
8. *Idea:* Gran and Grandpa's house

SECTION 11

1. *Idea:* Because they never used the front door
2. *Idea:* That there was an attic in the house
3. *Idea:* To visit Mrs. Hawkins
4. *Idea:* Fishing
5. *Idea:* To find where the wall sounded hollow
6. *Idea:* Great-Uncle John's
7. *Idea:* So he could get away from his brother and sister
8. No
9. *Idea:* Great-Uncle John's seashell collection
10. *Idea:* Aunt Mary's needlepoint bag
11. *Idea:* Grandpa's ship model

Bibliography of Correlated Trade Literature

Bibliography of Correlated Trade Literature

Note: Check the appropriateness of the vocabulary before making any selection for students to read independently.

Selection	Suggested Theme	Correlated Literature
Old Henry *Henry Meets Tim* *Tim's Questions* *Tim Has a Flying Lesson* *Tim Practices Flying* *The Geese Leave Big Trout Lake* *Old Henry Tests Tim* *A New Plan* *Flying with the Flock* *The Flock Reaches Florida* *Back to Canada* (Lessons 1–12)	Animal Adventures	• Betancourt, Jeanne **Ten True Animal Rescues**—NF • Burnford, Sheila **The Incredible Journey**—F • Byars, Betsy **The Midnight Fox**—F • Curwood, James Oliver **Baree: The Story of a Wolf-Dog**—F • Wallace, Bill **Red Dog**—F • Weaver, Harriet E. **Frosty: A Raccoon to Remember and Indomitable**—NF
Oomoo *Usk, the Polar Bear* *Playing with Usk* *The Beach* *The Ice Floe* *Drifting on an Ice Chunk* *The Storm* *The Killer Whales Wait* *Usk and the Killer Whale* (Lessons 13–22)	Young and Brave	• MacLachlan, Patricia **Sarah, Plain and Tall**—F • Rosen, Michael J. **The Heart Is Big Enough: Five Stories**—F • Sperry, Armstrong **Call It Courage**—F, SP • Uchida, Yoshiko **Journey to Topaz**—F • Wilder, Laura Ingalls **Little House in the Big Woods**—F

F: Fiction   FO: Folktales/Fables   NF: Nonfiction   PI: Picture Book   PL: Play   PO: Poetry
*Supplementary Novel SP: Available in Spanish

Bibliography of Correlated Trade Literature

Note: Check the appropriateness of the vocabulary before making any selection for students to read independently.

Selection	Suggested Theme	Correlated Literature
Dinosaurs *Edna Parker* *Looking for Something to Do* *The Lifeboat* *A Giant Whirlpool* *A Long Night* *Footprints* *The Monster* *Looking for Carla* *Explosion* *Back in the Lifeboat* *Saved* (Lessons 23–35)	Monsters: Real and Imaginary	• Arnold, Caroline ***Giant Shark: Megalodon, Prehistoric Super Predator***—NF • Butterworth, Oliver ***The Enormous Egg***—F • Moss, Jeffrey ***Bone Poems***—PO • Pringle, Laurence ***Animal Monsters: The Truth About Scary Creatures***—NF
Grandmother Esther *Grandmother Esther's Inventions* *Trying to Discover Needs* *Bad Ideas* *A Plan for Inventing* *The Electric Eye* *A Good Idea* *One Way* *Another Problem* *Leonard's Model* *An Invention Fair* *The Manufacturers at the Fair* *Deals* *The First-Prize Winner* *Your Turn* (Lessons 36–52)	Inventions and Inventors	• Fritz, Jean ***What's the Big Idea, Ben Franklin?***—NF • Getz, David ***Almost Famous***—F • Matthews, Tom and Gilbert Grosvenor ***Always Inventing*** NF • McPherson, Stephanie Sammartino ***TV's Forgotten Hero: The Story of Philo Farnsworth***—NF • Reynolds, Quentin ***The Wright Brothers: Pioneers of American Aviation***—NF • Sullivan, Otha Richard and James Haskins ***African American Inventors***—NF

F: Fiction   FO: Folktales/Fables   NF: Nonfiction   PI: Picture Book   PL: Play   PO: Poetry
*Supplementary Novel SP: Available in Spanish

Bibliography of Correlated Trade Literature

Note: Check the appropriateness of the vocabulary before making any selection for students to read independently.

Selection	Suggested Theme	Correlated Literature

An Important Test
The Test Questions
Waiting for a Letter
A Surprise at the Space Station
Traveler Four
The Gravity Device
Jupiter
Io
The Space Station on Io
A Trip to the Volcano
Help
Sidney
Back to Earth
(Lessons 53–66)
	Out of This World	• Couper, Heather and Nigel Henbest
		  Is Anybody Out There?—NF
		
		• Coville, Bruce
		  I Left My Sneakers in Dimension X—F
		
		• Kettelkamp, Larry
		  Living in Space—NF
		
		• Lauber, Patricia
		  Journey to the Planets—NF
		
		• Schraff, Anne E.
		  Are We Moving to Mars?—NF
		
		• Spinner, Stephanie and Terry Bisson
		  Be First in the Universe—F

Waldo's Cooking
A Problem
Waldo Gets a Job
The Pet Shop
Maria and Waldo Make a Deal
Waldo Starts Training Animals
The Animal Show
A Big Crowd
Problems at the Pet Shop
Changing the Rewards
New Rewards and a New Super Trick
A Great Show
Plans for a Trip
On the Tour
The Pyramid
The Animals' Greatest Show
(Lessons 67–84)
	First Jobs	• Bulla, Clyde Robert
		  Shoeshine Girl—F
		
		• Cleary, Beverly
		  Henry and the Paper Route—F
		
		• Danziger, Paula
		  Not for a Billion Gazillion Dollars—F
		
		• McQuinn, Conn
		  Kidbiz: Everything You Need to Start Your Own Business—NF
		
		• Naylor, Phyllis Reynolds
		  Eddie, Incorporated—F
		
		• Robertson, Keith
		  Henry Reed's Baby-Sitting Service—F

F: Fiction   FO: Folktales/Fables   NF: Nonfiction   PI: Picture Book   PL: Play   PO: Poetry
*Supplementary Novel SP: Available in Spanish

Bibliography of Correlated Trade Literature

Note: Check the appropriateness of the vocabulary before making any selection for students to read independently.

Selection	Suggested Theme	Correlated Literature
Darla's Fear *Getting Ready to Dive* *An Underwater World* *An Emergency* *The Trip to the Water's Surface* (Lessons 85–89)	Underwater Adventures	• Gibbons, Gail ***Sunken Treasure***—NF • Grover, Wayne ***Dolphin Treasure***—NF • Suranna, Keith ***20,000 Leagues Under the Sea***—PL • Woodman, Nancy ***Sea-Fari Deep***—NF
Susie and Denali *Getting Ready for a Run* *A Practice Run* *Examination Day* *The Big Race* *On the Trail* *Lost* *Beware of Streams* *End of the Race* (Lessons 91–99)	Big Races	• Bledsoe, Lucy Jane ***The Big Bike Race***—F • Climo, Shirley ***Atalanta's Race: A Greek Myth***—FO • Gardiner, John Reynolds ***Stone Fox***—F • O'Dell, Scott ***Black Star, Bright Dawn***—F • Platt, Chris ***Willow King: Race the Wind***—F

F: Fiction   FO: Folktales/Fables   NF: Nonfiction   PI: Picture Book   PL: Play   PO: Poetry
*Supplementary Novel SP: Available in Spanish

Note: Check the appropriateness of the vocabulary before making any selection for students to read independently.

Selection	Suggested Theme	Correlated Literature

Go Anywhere—See Anything
The First Trip
Al Learns More About Speed
Al Takes a Test About Speed
Al Learns About Matter
Al Visits Saturn and Pluto
Al Takes a Test About Matter
Al Takes Another Test
Al Learns About Molecules
Al Learns More About
   Molecules
Al Takes a Test About
   Molecules
Angela Meets the Old Man
Angela and Al Learn About
   Water Pressure
Deep-Sea Critters
Al and Angela See Strange
   Sea Animals
Al and Angela Go to the
   Bottom of the Ocean
A Test About the Ocean
Angela and Al See Our
   Galaxy
Angela and Al Learn About
   Muscles
Al and Angela Learn About
   Bones
Angela and Al Learn About
   the Heart
Al and Angela Follow Blood
   Through the Body
Angela and Al Learn About
   Nerves
Al and Angela Learn About
   the Brain
Angela and Al Learn About
   the Eye
Al and Angela Learn About
   the Ear
Angela and Al Study for a
   Test
	Exploration and Discovery	• Davidson, Margaret
		  Louis Braille: The Boy Who
		  Invented Books for the
		  Blind— NF
		
		• DuBois, William Pene
		  The Twenty-One Balloons—F
		
		• Kimmel, Elizabeth Cody
		  Ice Story: Shackleton's Lost
		  Expedition—NF
		
		• Lindgren, Astrid
		  Pippi Longstocking—F
		
		• Steffof, Rebecca
		  Extraordinary Explorers:
		  Scientific Explorers, Women
		  of the World, Accidental
		  Explorers—NF

F: Fiction   FO: Folktales/Fables   NF: Nonfiction   PI: Picture Book   PL: Play   PO: Poetry
*Supplementary Novel SP: Available in Spanish

Bibliography of Correlated Trade Literature

Note: Check the appropriateness of the vocabulary before making any selection for students to read independently.

Selection	Suggested Theme	Correlated Literature
Angela and Al Take a Test About the Human Body *Winter at the North Pole* *Angela and Al Learn About Snowflakes* *A Trip to the South Pole* *A Book About the Poles* *Angela and Al Buy Christmas Presents* *Angela and Al Go to the Library* *Angela and Al Read About Baboons* *Angela and Al Finish Their Last Trip* *Go Anywhere—See Anything with Books* (Lessons 101–139)	Exploration and Discovery (cont.)	

F: Fiction   FO: Folktales/Fables   NF: Nonfiction   PI: Picture Book   PL: Play   PO: Poetry
*Supplementary Novel SP: Available in Spanish

Little House on the Prairie
Laura Ingalls Wilder

Crossing the Creek

Little House on the Prairie tells the story of a close-knit pioneer family and their adventures in the western frontier territories of the United States in the 19th century. There is a whole collection of "Little House" books, and each is based on the true-life adventures of the author's real family. In this selection, the Ingalls family—Pa, Ma, Mary, Laura, and Carrie—has just left their home in the Big Woods of Wisconsin to settle further west. They are about to cross a creek in their covered wagon.

Laura was surprised because she did not see the creek. But the bottom lands were wide. Down here, below the prairie, there were gentle hills and open sunny places. The air was still and hot. Under the wagon wheels the ground was soft. In the sunny open spaces the grass grew thin, and deer had cropped it short.

For a while the high, bare cliffs of red earth stood up behind the wagon. But they were almost hidden behind hills and trees when Pet and Patty stopped to drink from the creek.

The rushing sound of the water filled the still air. All along the creek banks the trees hung over it and made it dark with shadows. In the middle it ran swiftly, sparkling silver and blue.

"This creek's pretty high," Pa said. "But I guess we can make it all right. You can see this is a ford, by the old wheel ruts. What do you say, Caroline?"

"Whatever you say, Charles," Ma answered.

Pet and Patty lifted their wet noses. They pricked their ears forward, looking at the creek; then they pricked them backward to hear what Pa would say. They sighed and laid their soft noses together to whisper to each other. A little way upstream, Jack was lapping the water with his red tongue.

"I'll tie down the wagon-cover," Pa said. He climbed down from the seat, unrolled the canvas sides and tied them firmly to the wagon-box. Then he pulled the rope at the back, so that the canvas puckered together in the middle, leaving only a tiny round hole, too small to see through.

Mary huddled down on the bed. She did not like fords; she was afraid of the rushing water. But Laura was excited; she liked the splashing. Pa climbed to the seat, saying, "They may have to swim, out there in the middle. But we'll make it alright, Caroline."

Laura thought of Jack and said, "I wish Jack could ride in the wagon, Pa."

Pa did not answer. He gathered the reins tightly in his hands. Ma said, "Jack can swim, Laura. He will be all right."

The wagon went forward softly in mud. Water began to splash against the wheels. The splashing grew louder. The wagon shook as the noisy water struck at it. Then all at once the wagon lifted and balanced and swayed. It was a lovely feeling.

The noise stopped, and Ma said, sharply, "Lie down, girls!"

Quick as a flash, Mary and Laura dropped flat on the bed. When Ma spoke like that, they did as they were told. Ma's arm pulled a smothering blanket over them, heads and all.

"Be still, just as you are. Don't move!" she said.

Mary did not move; she was trembling and still. But Laura could not help wriggling a little bit. She did so want to see what was happening. She could feel the wagon swaying and turning; the splashing was noisy again, and again it died away. Then Pa's voice frightened Laura. It said, "Take them, Caroline!"

The wagon lurched; there was a sudden heavy splash beside it. Laura sat straight up and clawed the blanket from her head.

Pa was gone. Ma sat alone, holding tight to the reins with both hands. Mary hid her face in the blanket again, but Laura rose up farther. She couldn't see the creek bank. She couldn't see anything in front of the wagon but water rushing at it. And in the water, three heads; Pet's head and Patty's head and Pa's small, wet head. Pa's fist in the water was holding tight to Pet's bridle.

Laura could faintly hear Pa's voice through the rushing of the water. It sounded calm and cheerful, but she couldn't hear what he said. He was talking to the horses. Ma's face was white and scared.

"Lie down, Laura," Ma said.

Laura lay down. She felt cold and sick. Her eyes were shut tight, but she could still see the terrible water and Pa's brown beard drowning in it.

For a long, long time the wagon swayed and swung, and Mary cried without making a sound, and Laura's stomach felt sicker and sicker. Then the front wheels struck and grated, and Pa shouted. The whole wagon jerked and jolted and tipped backward, but the wheels were turning on the ground. Laura was up again, holding to the seat; she saw Pet's and Patty's scrambling wet backs climbing a steep bank, and Pa running beside them, shouting, "Hi, Patty! Hi, Pet! Get up! Get up! Whoopsy-daisy! Good girls!"

At the top of the bank they stood still, panting and dripping. And the wagon stood still, safely out of that creek.

Pa stood panting and dripping, too, and Ma said, "Oh, Charles!"

"There, there, Caroline," said Pa. "We're all safe, thanks to a good tight wagon-box well fastened to the running-gear. I never saw a creek rise so fast in my life. Pet and Patty are good swimmers, but I guess they wouldn't have made it if I hadn't helped them."

If Pa had not known what to do, or if Ma had been too frightened to drive, or if Laura and Mary had been naughty and bothered her, then they would all have been lost. The river would have rolled them over and over and carried them away and drowned them, and nobody would ever have known what became of them. For weeks, perhaps, no other person would come along that road.

"Well," said Pa, "all's well that ends well," and Ma said, "Charles, you're wet to the skin."

Before Pa could answer, Laura cried, "Oh, where's Jack?"

They had forgotten Jack. They had left him on the other side of that dreadful water and now they could not see him anywhere. He must have tried to swim after them, but they could not see him struggling in the water now.

Laura swallowed hard, to keep from crying. She knew it was shameful to cry, but there was crying inside her. All the long way from Wisconsin poor Jack had followed them so patiently and faithfully, and now they had left him to drown. He was so tired, and they might have taken him into the wagon. He had stood on the bank and seen the wagon going away from him, as if they didn't care for him at all. And he would never know how much they wanted him.

Pa said he wouldn't have done such a thing to Jack, not for a million dollars. If he'd known how that creek would rise when they were in midstream, he would never have let Jack try to swim it.

"But that can't be helped now," he said.

He went far up and down the creek bank, looking for Jack, calling him and whistling for him.

It was no use. Jack was gone.

At last there was nothing to do but to go on. Pet and Patty were rested. Pa's clothes had dried on him while he searched for Jack. He took the reins again, and drove uphill, out of the river bottoms.

Laura looked back all the way. She knew she wouldn't see Jack again, but she wanted to. She didn't see anything but low curves of land coming between the wagon and the creek, and beyond the creek those strange cliffs of red earth rose up again.

Then other bluffs just like them stood up in front of the wagon. Faint wheel tracks went into a crack between those earthen walls. Pet and Patty climbed till the crack became a small grassy valley. And the valley widened out to the High Prairie once more.

No road, not even the faintest trace of wheels or of a rider's passing, could be seen anywhere. That prairie looked as if no human eye had ever seen it before. Only the tall wild grass covered the endless empty land and a great empty sky arched over it. Far away the sun's edge ran a pale pink glow, and above the pink was yellow, and above that blue. Above the blue sky was no color at all. Purple shadows were gathering over the land, and the wind was mourning.

Pa stopped the mustangs. He and Ma got out of the wagon to make camp, and Mary and Laura climbed down to the ground, too.

"Oh, Ma," Laura begged. "Jack has gone to heaven, hasn't he? He was such a good dog, can't he go to heaven?"

Ma did not know what to answer, but Pa said: "Yes, Laura, he can. God that doesn't forget the sparrows won't leave a good dog like Jack out in the cold."

Laura felt only a little better. She was not happy. Pa did not whistle about his work as usual, and after a while he said, "And what we'll do in a wild country without a good watchdog I don't know."

Camp on the High Prairie

Pa made camp as usual. First, he unhitched and unharnessed Pet and Patty, and he put them on their picket-lines. Picket lines were long ropes fastened to iron pegs driven into the ground. The pegs were called picket-pins. When horses were on picket-lines they could eat all the grass that the long ropes would let them reach. But when Pet and Patty were put on them, the first thing they did was to lie down and roll back and forth and over. They rolled till the feeling of the harness was all gone from their backs.

While Pet and Patty were rolling, Pa pulled all the grass from a large, round space of ground. There was old, dead grass at the roots of the green grass, and Pa would take no chance of setting the prairie on fire. If fire once started in that dry under-grass, it would sweep that whole country bare and black. Pa said, "Best be on the safe side, it saves trouble in the end."

When the space was clear of grass, Pa laid a handful of dry grass in its center. From the creek bottoms he brought an armful of twigs and dead wood. He laid small twigs and larger twigs and then the wood on the handful of dry grass, and he lighted the grass. The fire crackled merrily inside the ring of bare ground that it couldn't get out of.

Then Pa brought water from the creek, while Mary and Laura helped Ma get supper. Ma measured coffee beans into the coffee-mill and Mary ground them. Laura filled the coffee-pot with the water Pa brought, and Ma set the pot in the coals. She set the iron bake-oven in the coals, too.

While it heated, she mixed cornmeal and salt with water and patted it into little cakes. She greased the bake-oven with a pork-rind, laid the cornmeal cakes in it, and put on its iron cover. Then Pa raked more coals over the cover, while Ma sliced fat salt pork. She fried the slices in the iron spider. The spider had short legs to stand on in the coals, and that was why it was called a spider. If it had had no legs, it would have been only a frying pan.

The coffee boiled, the cakes baked, the meat fried, and they all smelled so good that Laura grew hungrier and hungrier.

Pa set the wagon-seat near the fire. He and Ma sat on it. Mary and Laura sat on the wagon tongue. Each of them had a tin plate, and a steel knife and a steel fork with white bone handles. Ma had a tin cup and Pa had a tin cup, and Baby Carrie had a little one all her own, but Mary and Laura had to share their tin cup. They drank water. They could not drink coffee until they grew up.

While they were eating supper the purple shadows closed around the camp fire. The vast prairie was dark and still. Only the wind moved stealthily through the grass, and the large, low stars hung glittering from the great sky.

The camp fire was cozy in the big, chill darkness. The slices of pork were crisp and fat, the corncakes were good. In the dark beyond the wagon, Pet and Patty were eating, too. They bit off bites of grass with sharply crunching sounds.

"We'll camp here a day or two," said Pa. "Maybe we'll stay here. There's good land, timber in the bottoms, plenty of game—everything a man could want. What do you say, Caroline?"

"We might go farther and fare worse," Ma replied.

"Anyway, I'll look around tomorrow," Pa said. "I'll take my gun and get us some good fresh meat."

He lighted his pipe with a hot coal and stretched out his legs comfortably. The warm, brown smell of tobacco smoke mixed with the warmth of the fire. Mary yawned, and slid off the wagon tongue to sit on the grass. Laura yawned, too. Ma quickly washed the tin plates, the tin cups, the knives and forks. She washed the bake-oven and the spider, and rinsed the dish-cloth.

For an instant she was still, listening to the long, wailing howl from the dark prairie. They all knew what it was. But that sound always ran cold up Laura's backbone and crinkled over the back of her head.

Ma shook the dish-cloth, and then she walked into the dark and spread the cloth on the tall grass to dry. When she came back Pa said: "Wolves. Half a mile away, I'd judge. Well, where there's deer there will be wolves. I wish—"

He didn't say what he wished, but Laura knew. He wished Jack were there. When wolves howled in the Big Woods, Laura had always known that Jack would not let them hurt her. A lump swelled hard in her throat and her nose smarted. She winked fast and did not cry. That wolf, or perhaps another wolf, howled again.

"Bedtime for little girls!" Ma said, cheerfully. Mary got up and turned around so that Ma could unbutton her. But Laura jumped up and stood still. She saw something. Deep in the dark beyond the firelight, two green lights were shining near the ground. They were eyes.

Cold ran up Laura's backbone, her scalp crinkled, her hair stood up. The green lights moved; one winked out, then the other winked out, then both shone steadily, coming nearer. Very rapidly they were coming nearer.

"Look Pa, look!" Laura said. "A wolf!"

Pa did not seem to move quickly, but he did. In an instant he took his gun out of the wagon and was ready to fire at those green eyes. The eyes stopped coming. They were still in the dark, looking at him.

"It can't be a wolf. Unless it's a mad wolf," Pa said. Ma lifted Mary into the wagon. "And it's not that," said Pa. "Listen to the horses." Pet and Patty were still biting off bits of grass.

"A lynx?" said Ma.

"Or a coyote?" Pa picked up a stick of wood; he shouted, and threw it. The green eyes went close to the ground, as if the animal crouched to spring. Pa held the gun ready. The creature did not move.

"Don't, Charles," Ma said. But Pa slowly walked toward those eyes. And slowly along the ground the eyes crawled toward him. Laura could see the animal in the edge of the dark. It was a tawny animal and brindled. Then Pa shouted and Laura screamed.

The next thing she knew she was trying to hug a jumping, panting, wriggling Jack, who lapped her face and hands with his warm wet tongue. She couldn't hold him. He leaped and wriggled from her to Pa to Ma and back to her again.

"Well, I'm beat!" Pa said.

"So am I," said Ma. "But did you have to wake the baby?" She rocked Carrie in her arms, hushing her.

Jack was perfectly well. But soon he lay down close to Laura and sighed a long sigh. His eyes were red with tiredness, and all the under part of him was caked with mud. Ma gave him a cornmeal cake and he licked it and wagged politely, but he could not eat. He was too tired.

"No telling how long he kept swimming," Pa said. "Nor how far he was carried downstream before he landed," And when at last he reached them, Laura called him a wolf, and Pa threatened to shoot him.

But Jack knew they didn't mean it. Laura asked him, "You knew we didn't mean it, didn't you, Jack?" Jack wagged his stump of a tail; he knew.

Julie Rescues Big Mack
Written by Roger Hall

Julie was on school patrol. She and her best friend, Becky, were always on patrol on Wednesdays.

Julie liked it best in the mornings because adults had to use the crossing on their way to work. Adults know they should obey the traffic patrol monitors so as to set a good example to the children. But they often talked to Julie while they waited for the traffic to be stopped.

Mr. Mason came down the street.

"Morning, Mr. Mason," said Julie.

Mr. Mason had his big German shepherd dog with him. His name was Mack, and everyone called him Big Mack, after the hamburgers.

Julie had always wanted a dog of her own, but her dad wouldn't let her have one.

"Dogs are a nuisance . . . feeding them, exercising them, and getting someone to look after them when we go away," he would say. "Besides, they take up room in the car."

Also, Julie's little brother, Jason, was allergic to dogs.

Having a dog in the car was one of the reasons why Julie wanted a dog. She loved seeing how dogs stuck their heads out of the windows, always eager to see where they were going.

She liked it on patrol when she stopped builders' trucks, because the trucks often had dogs on the back.

When Mr. Mason stopped at the crossing, Big Mack would always sit until given the signal to cross. He was a beautifully trained dog. Mr. Mason had taken him to classes.

"When you have a dog like this," Mr. Mason said to Julie, "you have to make sure you can control him. If a dog behaves badly, it's usually the fault of the owner."

Julie got books out of the library about looking after and training dogs. She wanted to know what were the right things to do, just in case something amazing happened and she suddenly had a dog to look after.

On Wednesday, after school, Becky delivered the free newspaper, and sometimes she and Julie would go through the paper together, reading all about the local events.

Julie liked looking at the part of the paper that featured the 'Pet of the Week.' This was a photo, put in by the Animal Shelter, of a dog or a cat that needed a new home.

The cats usually managed to look quite cheerful, but the dogs always looked sad. No wonder, because the caption underneath often said something like, 'Sammy is a ten-month cross terrier. If Sammy doesn't find a home soon, he will have to be put to sleep.'

Julie knew what 'put to sleep' meant, and she didn't like to think of it. How *could* her father say 'no' to giving a home to all those sad dogs.

Sometimes, she would go up to the Animal Shelter to look at the dogs and to talk to them. They were always grateful for some attention. Sometimes Mrs. Rendell, the lady who ran the Shelter, would let Julie help her.

One morning, Mr. Mason came to the crossing by himself.

"Where's Big Mack?" asked Julie.

Mr. Mason looked very sad—almost sadder than the Pet of the Week.

"He's been stolen," Mr. Mason said. "I left him outside the supermarket for a few minutes, and when I came back, he was gone. Mack wouldn't run away. He's too well trained."

"Why would anyone want to steal Big Mack?" asked Julie.

Mr. Mason shook his head and shrugged. "I only wish I knew where to start looking for him."

During school that day, Julie could hardly pay attention. She was thinking about Mack being stolen, and about poor Mr. Mason being upset.

Then she imagined herself discovering the thief, and stepping up bravely, saying, "That is not your dog! That is Big Mack, and I know who he belongs to!"

A week later, when Julie was on crossing duty again, Mr. Mason told her he still had no news about Big Mack. He looked sadder than ever. Julie thought that what he needed was another dog, and she decided to go up to the Animal Shelter that afternoon after school.

When she got within a few blocks of the Shelter, Julie suddenly heard a long, sad howl coming from a rickety barn, almost hidden from the road. It was the saddest sound she had ever heard.

No on seemed to be around the old barn, so she crept up to the window and tried to look in.

The window was too dusty to be able to see anything, but Julie knew that there was a very sad animal in there.

She had to do something. She tried the door, but it was locked up tight.

Then an idea popped into Julie's head. She turned and ran the two blocks to the Animal Shelter, and told Mrs. Rendell about what she had heard.

Mrs. Rendell said, "Well, we'll have to check into that."

She called in Ross, the van driver, whose job it was to investigate reports of animal neglect.

He and Julie jumped in the van and drove to the old barn.

By the time they got there, the howling and wailing was even louder. Ross pried the door open, and there in the corner, in a wire cage, was a very big dog. The dog was very thin, and its fur was matted and dirty.

As Julie stepped closer, she suddenly saw that this was not just any dog—it was Big Mack!

Big Mack wagged his tail and tried to lick her through the wire mesh. He was really a mess, with cuts on his leg and across his back. "Poor Mack! What happened to you?"

"He was probably stolen by one of those dog-fight gangs," said Ross. "They take big, fierce dogs like this, and make them fight other dogs. People will pay to see that sort of thing. Very sad." Ross shook his head.

"But Big Mack isn't a fierce dog! He's very sweet and gentle," Julie said, and she gave the dog a hug through the walls of the cage.

They got Big Mack out of the cage, and Ross carried him to the van. Big Mack was too weak to walk, but he panted happily as Julie held his head.

At the Animal Shelter, the vet checked Big Mack out to make sure he was alright, and Julie ran to the phone.

"Mr. Mason, I'm down at the Animal Shelter, and there's a dog here I think you would like to see."

"Oh, I don't know, Julie . . . I don't think there could ever be another Big Mack," sighed Mr. Mason.

"Please, just come and see. I think you'll be surprised." Julie could hardly keep from blurting out her surprise.

Mr. Mason said he would come down to the Shelter right away.

When Mr. Mason walked through the door, there was Big Mack waiting for him. He couldn't run to his master, but he did wag his tail wildly.

"Mack! My big boy! Where did you find him?" He hugged Big Mack and Julie in the same hug.

Julie told Mr. Mason the story, and then the vet filled him in on Big Mack's condition. The dog had been badly mistreated, but he was in good enough shape to go home. Mr. Mason and Julie helped Big Mack limp out to the car, and then they headed home.

When the car pulled up to Julie's house, Mr. Mason said, "Julie, I really don't know how to thank you. I know how much you want a dog of your own."

"Yes," said Julie, eagerly.

"And I know you can't have one because of your brother," continued Mr. Mason. "But if you like you can come and visit Mack any time you want. You can take him for walks, and groom him, and bathe him."

"I could be his aunt," said Julie.

"That's a very good description," said Mr. Mason.

ACKNOWLEDGMENTS

Grateful acknowledgment is given to the following publishers and copyright owners for permissions granted to reprint selections from their publications. All possible care has been taken to trace ownership and secure permission for each selection included. In case of any errors or omissions, the Publisher will be pleased to make suitable acknowledgments in future editions.

HarperCollins
"Crossing the Creek" and "Camp on High Prairie" from LITTLE HOUSE ON THE PRAIRIE by Laura Ingalls Wilder. TEXT COPYRIGHT 1935, 1963 Little House Heritage Trust. Used by permission of HarperCollins Publishers.

Thomson Learning Australia
JULIE RESCUES BIG MACK by Roger Hall used by permission of Thomson Learning Australia.

ACKNOWLEDGMENTS

Grateful acknowledgment is given to the following publishers and copyright owners for permissions granted to reprint selections from their publications. All possible care has been taken to trace ownership and secure permission for each selection included. In case of any errors or omissions, the Publisher will be pleased to make suitable acknowledgments in future editions.

HarperCollins
"Crossing the Creek" and "Camp on High Prairie" from LITTLE HOUSE ON THE PRAIRIE by Laura Ingalls Wilder. TEXT COPYRIGHT 1935, 1963 Little House Heritage Trust. Used by permission of HarperCollins Publishers.

Thomson Learning Australia
JULIE RESCUES BIG MACK by Roger Hall used by permission of Thomson Learning Australia.